FARE EV

LONDON's BUSES

Catch you? Yes we can!

RON GWILLIAM

Design, typesetting and publishing by UK Book Publishing

www.ukbookpublishing.com

ISBN: 978-1-916572-69-0

FARE EVASION ON
LONDON's
BUSES

Catch you? Yes we can!

Disciplaimer

The information contained in this publication is based upon my own career, experiences, memories, research and ephemera. Under no circumstances must it be assumed that any views or comments herein are endorsed by London Transport (TfL) and none is intended.

TfL Internal bulletin

26 MARCH 2015

For those of you that are not aware, Ron Gwilliam has decided to take his retirement from 18 April 2015 after almost 40 years' service and is currently the longest serving employee in EOS. Ron started as a bus conductor at Tottenham Garage on 11 August 1975. He was the last night conductor on the buses. He became an RPI in 1984 when everything was done manually. He went on to become a Plain Clothes Official, worked on the Security Squad, became a Senior Revenue Protection Inspector (SRPI), Assistant Revenue Protection Manager for NE area, a Night Supervisor and additionally, an RPI Instructor, IPS Investigator and Court Presenter then his current role as Operational Supervisor. Ron has played a major role within revenue protection over the years and many of the things that you see in the role today has a touch of influence from Ron. I would like to thank Ron for the service he has given to TfL and wish him all the best in his retirement.

Steve Burton
EOS Director (Head of Bus Enforcement)

Dedication

During my 40 years on London Transport (TfL) I worked with an incalculable number of colleagues in a number of various roles. But this publication is dedicated to the following six individuals;

Michael (Mick) Hawkins: Who was the first of these individuals I encountered when I became a night bus conductor. Mick was a night Inspector (who went on to become the Central Area night manager) and we were both 'Spurs' supporters. We quickly found a common cause for discussion, apart from, where Mick might appear from out of nowhere along the route to make sure my driver and I were running to time.

Jess Nash: For many years my on-road 'Checking Buddy' who was also a wonderful source of advice and comfort during a very turbulent time in my life. Jess became not only a wonderful friend but also an extended part of my family.

Rod Dixon: A conductor like myself at Tottenham Garage, who I later mentored in his ambition to become an RPI. Rod's hobby was photography and over the years photographed a number of family weddings (including my second). Like Jess, Rod and his lovely family became extended members of mine.

Alex Whitmey: Like me, Alex is Marmite. When we first encountered each other we both would gladly have 'Spread' the other over the top deck of a bus. Unbelievably, despite this inauspicious beginning, we soon came to realise that we had many things in common. One of which was a pride in our appearance. No matter how hard I tried, nobody did 'Smart' like Alex. He later became the 'Night Revenue Manager' and was responsible for changing night RPIs attire from plain clothes to uniform in an effort not only to improve the appearance of night bus ticket Inspectors but also on the grounds of health and safety. This change meant it was far easier to keep an eye on his staff on the top deck of a crowded and often rowdy night bus.

William (Billy) Mair: An outspoken Scot who didn't suffer fools easily, including managers. When I first took over Billy's team many people predicted sparks would soon fly. Billy was king of the one-liners such as 'You never get a second chance to make a first impression' or, when I might be giving a team talk for example, would say 'You're a good act Ron, but you've been on too long.' He had a few others I'll not commit to print.

Martin Brogan: One of my last, young, new recruits. Martin was keen to know not only why TfL and London Transport had certain working practices and procedures but also why I ran my team the way I did. I started to become suspicious that Martin was a management 'Plant' to see if I was still embracing the company's evolving ethos despite my 'Old School' tag. I need not have worried.

To all of these individuals, I would like to thank you for your loyal and lasting friendship.

Introduction

Since I retired in 2015 after spending the best part of 40 years selling and checking tickets for London Transport as both a day and night bus conductor and later a Revenue Protection Inspector (RPI) starting on 11 August 1975, I have been asked a few times, by those interested in such things, when ticket Inspectors were first employed by London Transport or its predecessors. I assume that some of these individuals who were often a lot younger than me clearly believed that I was also responsible for feeding the horses at bus terminals. My reason for committing this to print is that I discovered that there is, to my knowledge, very little information on this subject. It has, however, proved to be a far more difficult question to conclusively answer than I imagined. I have even enlisted the assistance of the London Transport Museum who provided a number of interesting facts and articles but even they have been unable to give a definitive answer. Because of this I quickly realised that there is a vacuum of information or knowledge available with regards to what has been a fascinating, varied and much misunderstood profession. It also occurred to me that I was fortunate to have been employed in revenue protection duties during the years following my early predecessors, whose main function was collecting and accounting for cash only tickets, and just before and during the introduction of a plethora of bus passes, capital cards and travelcards which would ultimately result in an explosion of fare evasion opportunities for the travelling public. Now, for the first time, in view of the fact that due to modern-day travel documents and structures, none of the examples I am about to reveal can ever be exploited again, you can learn all the tricks, scams and fiddles that many of London's bus passengers and some unscrupulous members of staff devised to either evade paying their fare or avoid getting caught with their fingers in the 'proverbial' till or in this case 'cash tray.' I will also reveal the tactics, practices, and procedures employed by London Transport Revenue Staff to detect and deter these nefarious activities.

However, it is only right that before we embark on a journey together around London by bus and encountering these activities, that you grasp the fundamentals of what was required and expected of London's bus drivers, conductors and Revenue Protection Inspectors at that time.

Author, 1987

Catch you? Yes we can!

M y intention is not to over-burden the reader, whether they be current employees, ex-staff or the general public, with regulations, dates or statistics but rather my experiences and memories of life in my everyday encounters with bus drivers, conductors and passengers whose often ingenious and sometimes lamentable, not to say laughable, ploys to steal company money or evade paying their fare may well surprise and amuse a great number of people. The introduction of oyster and credit card payment systems and the complete withdrawal of printed passes (with the exception of the one-day travelcard) and cash tickets has finally put an end to the visual detection skills that were, as you will come to appreciate in the following accounts, a highly developed technique. Sadly today, RPIs' are totally dependent on a 'RID' (revenue inspection device) that reads the oyster or credit card, even those stored on smartphones or watches, and should this device fail to function they are unable to accurately continue ticket checking duties. Lastly, a quick outline surrounding the question that has me stumped should help the reader grasp the background to the early evolution of a ticket inspector on London's buses.

Put simply, the early days of unregulated bus travel was a somewhat complicated affair with regards to how fares were collected and accounted for by conductors. To begin with no tickets were issued by conductors who merely had to record on their waybill how many passengers entered the bus on each journey. From this the bus companies worked out how much money should have been collected and paid in, due to a flat-fare system. The first recorded reference to Inspectors was in 1855 when 'Spots' were employed by the London General Omnibus Company to ride buses and check that conductors were recording the correct number of passengers that had boarded on that particular journey. This changed in 1891 when roll-type tickets were introduced. From my own recollection I can confirm that in the mid to late 50's my mum would often take us kids shopping by bus and ticket inspectors wearing black uniforms were a familiar sight. That leaves an awful long period of time unaccounted for in-between. But let's not get too bogged-down here and leave that to other far more knowledgeable scholars in stats and facts. This publication is in no-way intended to be an indisputable history of Revenue Protection on London Transport buses.

Therefore, my story starts post October 1984 after my initial four-week classroom Revenue Protection Inspector training at Chiswick Works, the home of the World famous 'Skid Pan.' There followed a further four weeks 'On the Road' training with my RPI Instructor whom I was detailed to meet at the old Walthamstow bus garage which now, sadly, no longer exist.

On the road

As I prepare to leave home for a day on-the-road as a London Transport Revenue Protection Inspector (RPI) or, in plain English, ticket Inspector, there's just time for one last check of the equipment that I am going to need to allow me to do my job. Two black-ink and one red ink ball-point pens and two rubber-tipped pencils, *check*. Notebook, *check*. Duty statement and Area Duty frame, *check*. Fare charts and Credit notes, *check*. My photo ID and badge (commonly known as 'Plate') *check*. Over time this checklist would grow to include items such as, TATTS (Temporary Authority to Travel), Penalty Fare book, mobile phone, Cognito (electronic data devise), assault alarm, Spit Kit and body camera. Finally, one last look in the mirror to satisfy myself that my black uniform which consisted of blazer-style jacket and trousers (both lightweight and heavyweight for summer and winter) and crisp white shirt are clean and tidy, pressed to the highest standard and that the peak of my cap and black shoes (which we were not issued with at this time) are gleaming. In addition to these, male RPIs' were also issued with black clip-on ties (to prevent an aggressive passenger attempting to choke us) waistcoats and Crombie-style overcoats. The buttons on the jackets were regular black buttons but those on the overcoat each had an embossed 'Griffin'. Female RPIs' were issued with 'Bowler-style' hats, cravats and either trousers or skirts. Prior to 1984, the year I became an RPI, all ticket checking duties were conducted in uniform but that year it was decided that there was a need for plain-clothes checking duties and these were soon introduced to the rota. The only revenue staff that operated in plain clothes prior to this were 'Spots.' These officials would be sent out to ride on buses as passengers and observe members of staff who may be failing to correctly issue tickets in respect of the fares that were being paid by passengers, or in other words, in some cases, blatantly 'fiddling.'

My Area Duty Frame would indicate which area or routes I would be checking that day and I would be expected to plan my journey to reach these areas or routes as quickly as possible. There were no set quotas in those days however RPIs' were expected to check as many buses as they could and between 25 to 30 buses was considered achievable providing there were no unforeseen delays or incidents. One of the most attractive conditions of the job at that time was that you could start and finish duty at the nearest bus stop to your home. We worked a thirty-seven-and-a-half-hour week and each daily duty was seven hours and twenty-four minutes with an unpaid 'Meal-Relief' of thirty minutes in between, making a total time of 7hrs 54mins on the road. During the course of our duty, RPIs' were allowed to take a couple of duty breaks, commonly known as 'short reliefs or S/Rs for toilet purposes or tea breaks. These breaks, however, were not to be taken during the 'Rush-Hours,' which were between 7am to 9am or 4pm to 7pm Monday to Friday. Having reached our checking area or routes we were expected to spend as long as possible in that area and to plan our route back home to arrive as close to our finishing time as possible. The nature of our job meant that it was often not possible to time to the minute our arrival at our finishing point and therefore a 'Time in the Book' system was used that balanced out any plus or minus time on a daily basis meaning that if an RPI were to finish twenty minutes late they would aim to finish twenty minutes early the following working day, At this time, London and the surrounding suburbs, were divided into four checking areas which were, North East, North West, South East and South West. Each area covered a part of Central London closest to their boundaries. Some years later a Central Area and Night 'Squad' would be added. Each of these checking areas had approximately twenty RPIs' split into two equal 'Squads' numbered 1 & 2 to cover both early and late shifts. I was a north east (NE) RPI and assigned to Squad 2. When Squad 1 was on early shift, my squad would be on late shift and vice versa and this would rotate each week. Whilst in the designated checking area you would be required to meet your Squad leader or 'Gold Badge', whose formal title was Senior Revenue Protection Inspector (SRPI). For a brief period of time LT introduced a higher grade of Chief Revenue Protection Inspector but this was soon discontinued. We RPIs' were 'Silver Badge.' The purpose of these meetings, which were held in either a local bus garage or café, was to hand in your previous day's duty statement and reports and collect any stationary (report pads/ duty statements/credit notes etc.) In addition to these you would be required to read any Revenue notices or circulars regarding ticketing updates or planed events and diversions involving local bus routes. It needs to be pointed out at this juncture that these were the days before hand-held electronic 'devices,' computers or mobile phones. All reports had to be hand-written and accompanied with two copies for which blue (cc) carbon copy paper (also issued) had to be placed between each page and was the precursor to the computer forwarding function. There was a time allowance for each report (that had to be written at home at the end of duty) which was 10 minutes for the first report and five minutes for every subsequent report irrespective of how many words or pages. It was extremely frustrating if you had got four or five lines in on a report and realised you had omitted or misspelt something and had to 'bin it' and start again for which no further time could be claimed. 15 minutes was allowed to compile your duty statement which listed the time spent checking, total amount of buses/passengers checked and reports submitted including time claimed for report writing. The SPRI would take all the paperwork collected from RPIs' to the office where, prior to the days of computerisation, all these statistics and figures had to be manually recorded and each RPI's daily hours relayed to payrolls.

Rules

D rivers and conductors also known as 'Platform Staff' were required to carry out their duties as detailed in a book unsurprisingly entitled 'RULE BOOK for Drivers and Conductors.' There were 106 rules broken down into three sections as follows: **Part I** General rules, **Part II** Rules for Drivers, **Part III** Rules for Conductors. For the purposes of explanation, I will detail a few examples starting with; **Rule 1** which, (summed up in a few words), stated that all employees must make themselves familiar with and adhere to these rules and that ignorance of the rules will not be accepted for a failure to comply with them. *No pussy-footing around there then!* RPIs' were primarily concerned with enforcing revenue-related rules which covered rules 90 to 106 but could also report Platform staff for failure to comply with any of the rules set out.

A few examples for which an RPI could report a conductor are as follows: **B/R 90** (Breach of Rule 90) **Uncollected fare or fares,** which stated, (again in as few words as possible) that conductors must begin to collect fares as soon as passengers board the bus. Normally, conductors would be expected to have collected a passenger's fare within two or three stops of boarding and dependant on how busy the bus was when the

RPI boarded. Therefore, any passenger unable to offer a ticket for inspection would be asked where they had boarded and are travelling to, also if the conductor had been round to collect the fare. If deemed unacceptable and undisputed by the conductor (or proven by the RPI) then the fare would be collected, a ticket issued and the conductor reported. It was of course very easy for a passenger who intended to avoid paying to allege that the conductor had not been round to collect fares. However, if the conductor disputed this it was possible for an RPI to disprove this allegation by checking one or two passengers seated beyond this passenger and who had boarded after and were in possession of valid tickets.

On now to: **B/R 96 Uncollected excess fare or fares.** Conductors were expected to have ascertained how far a passenger wished to travel when first purchasing a ticket. If the passenger then remained on the bus beyond their stated destination the conductor was expected to have remembered and collected an excess fare and issued the passenger another ticket. Conductors were required to have a good memory and make frequent rounds of each deck.

B/R 7 Wearing of Uniform and Badges. This rule also covered how a conductor should wear their 'webbing' which referred to the straps which held the ticket machine. The webbing/straps should be outside (i.e., over the top) of the uniform jacket and not underneath. The reason for this is so that the ticket machine was fully visible at all times. The importance of this will become all the more obvious when we get to the section that deals with 'Spots' and their need to clearly observe and satisfy themselves that the conductor is not setting the machine to a lower value than that paid by the passenger. Also included in the rule book was a section pertaining to PSV (Public Service Vehicle) regulations with which drivers and conductors were also required to familiarise themselves.

Conductors

C onductor operated double-deck buses were, without a shadow of doubt, the most difficult buses to ticket check and the conductor the most difficult member of platform staff to covertly observe for a number of reasons as will become apparent in the following sections. Apart from supervising the safe boarding and alighting of passengers as well as giving the driver the starting signal (ringing off) from the platform the conductor was free to wander around the bus at will. This made covert observations by 'Spots' extremely difficult and this will be covered in greater detail later. To assist RPIs when carrying out ticket inspections a number of rules and instructions were issued to which the conductor was required to adhere to.

Rule 77: Known as *Position of Conductor* stated; Conductors must never remain inside the lower deck or on the upper deck of their buses longer than is necessary for collecting fares or answering enquiries etc. However, this was not always complied with for a number of reasons, some reasonable, understandable and innocent, others due to ignorance, laziness or nefarious intentions. One of the former reasons could be due to inclement weather when to spend long periods of time standing on the platform of an open-back (Routemaster) bus was very unappealing. When an RPI boarded the bus, conductors were expected to complete the transaction that they were engaged in and return to the platform. The RPI would ask the conductor for his/her waybill which would indicate the total register number on the ticket machine at the start of that journey. The RPI would then check the total register number on the machine indicating how many tickets had been sold up to this point and that the machine number matched that also recorded on the waybill. The RPI would now give one of two instructions to the conductor.

One would be to follow the RPI around the bus as he/she carried out their inspection. The other would be to remain on the platform until the inspection was complete. These instructions were to prevent an unscrupulous conductor from moving around the bus, collecting, for example, any previously uncollected fares. This could be due to laziness or perhaps having a friend or family member being allowed to travel free. Another 'Trick' that an unscrupulous conductor was prone to employ was to deliberately not collect fares and stand for long periods of time on the platform in the hope that a number of honest passengers would offer the conductor the fare as they left the bus (often in a rush to catch a train or connection) and would not wait for the conductor to issue them with a ticket. Another reason for scurrying around the bus could be that the conductor had issued a passenger a ticket for a lower amount than that paid. It was surprising how many passengers would not bother to check the ticket before putting it their pocket or purse. This was made an even more appealing 'opportunity' when 'Alpha' codes were introduced on ticket machines instead of numerals. Some conductors were known to pick up tickets left on the seat by passengers and re-issue this ticket to another passenger.

When inspecting passengers cash tickets an RPI would start by asking the passenger to confirm the amount of the fare requested. Many passengers would cheerfully comply, however, on occasions, some disgruntled or anti-authoritarian individuals would say "it tells you on the ticket, doesn't it" The reason for this question is that if the fare requested or paid was different to that printed on the ticket this would need to be further investigated. The next question would be to ask the passenger where they had boarded the bus. Again, many passengers would comply without complaint but our disgruntled passenger would often repeat "It tells you on the ticket, doesn't it." The third question would be to ask the passenger where they are travelling to. My reason for relating this procedure is that many passengers surmised that these questions were merely to ensure that they were not attempting to evade paying the correct fare or that the RPI was somewhat incompetent. The first was, of course, one reason. However, the second surmised reason was certainly not. The main reason was to ensure that the conductor or driver/operator had continued to set their ticket machines to record the correct fare stage boarded by the passenger and fare requested and paid. Should any of these not been confirmed then a number of irregularities may have been committed. An incorrect fare stage could indicate that the member of staff had merely been failing to carry out their duties diligently and could have caused the passenger some inconvenience and embarrassment if suspected of not paying the correct fare. It could also be that the ticket had in fact been issued to or for another passenger and had been 're-issued' with the possibility the member of staff had collected two fares in exchange for the same ticket. Another possibility is that the passenger may have picked up a ticket discarded by another passenger and had stated an incorrect boarding point which would raise suspicion and need to be investigated with the conductor. I would often politely point out to a passenger that made these comments in response to my questions, that a ticket cannot talk and my enquiries were simply to confirm that what was printed on the ticket was correct in relation to their intended journey.

Ticket machines

T he ticket machines in use at this time and which I used in all my nine years as a bus conductor was the famous 'Gibson' machine, so named after George Gibson, London Transport Superintendent of Fare Collections, based at the Effra Road ticket printing works in Brixton, and who had designed it. These heavy, metal, bull-nosed, machines were hand-powered and operated and were in service from 1953 until 21 August 1993 when they were phased out in favour of PETMs' (Portable Electronic Ticket Machines.) I will return to the mechanics of the Gibson ticket machine in more detail when describing the tactics employed by both the unscrupulous conductor and the 'Spots' in their intriguing battle of wits. One other more serious tactic employed/devised by conductors was when it was discovered that a Wolf electric drill could be inserted into a particular point in the casing of the Gibson ticket machine and the total register number could be re-wound or re-set. This could be done, for instance, when a conductor living near to the garage took the machine home on their meal-relief before returning to duty.

I wish to include, for two reasons, one particular incident from my own days as a conductor. The first: for information purposes. The second: for amusement. Many members of the public today would be well aware of the many types of bus passes, travelcards, elderly persons travel permits and saver-tickets, not to mention staff passes, which were valid for travel on London buses. But possibly the least known and rarest of all was the 'LT Medallion'. These Medallions were issued to senior members of London Transport such as Directors and Executives and were about the size of a ten pence piece which would usually be attached to a chain which the holder would place in a waistcoat pocket (much like a 'fob' or pocket watch). The obverse bore the words 'London Transport Executive' or 'London Transport Board' and bore a 'Griffin'. The reverse of this Medallion bore the word 'Pass' and would be engraved with the holder's name and number and was valid for unlimited travel on all London Transport services. Now, as far as the amusing part of this incident is concerned, the reader needs to know that on my first day as a conductor, my instructor told me that there were two golden rules (both unofficial) that all conductors abided by. The first was that you should never take the fare from a nurse travelling in uniform (in light of recent events this seems a far more rewarding gesture than standing on your doorstep clapping). The second was that you should never take a fare from a member of staff showing their staff pass and paying for a companion. In my naivety I happily followed these 'rules' and added them to the 106 official rules I was required to adhere to. Sometime after my training I was conducting a route 73 bus in Oxford Street when a stout, smartly-dressed middle-aged man, travelling with a young woman, boarded and sat together on the offside of the lower deck (you might take from this detailed positional information that what followed has remained firmly engraved in my memory… and you would be right). As I approached these passengers the male showed me his Medallion with his left hand and in his right hand had the fare for his companion which he offered. I waived this away saying, "Nah, that's alright mate" but before I could take more than two steps further into the lower deck, a deep, booming voice saying "No, it is *NOT*, alright" stopped me in my tracks. He handed me the fare and I issued him a ticket and continued with my duties. The man and his companion left the bus a few stops later and nothing more was said. I assumed that that would be the end of the matter but a couple of days later I was called into the manager's office and given a stern piece of advice and guidance. The next time I saw my conductor Instructor I mentioned this incident and said "Thanks for dropping me in it". He then gave me a further piece of advice, saying "I said, members of staff, not Directors and Executives, you idiot" Happy days.

In the days of cash only fares, the scale of opportunities for the travelling public to evade their fare on conductor operated buses was clearly very limited. One such tactic would be to pretend to be asleep. A conductor colleague of mine at Tottenham Garage had an amusing counter-tactic for passengers he suspected of doing this. He could imitate the sound of a wasp extremely convincingly. He would stand next to the passenger, perform his party- piece, and watch as the passenger would suddenly 'wake-up' making swatting movements around his head with his hands. The conductor would then smile innocently whilst casually saying 'anymore fares?' Sadly, I never actually saw him perform this strategy.

The most common and apparently innocent way to avoid paying a fare would be to tender a high value note in the hope that the conductor would not have enough change, especially early in the mornings, when the conductor was likely to not have taken enough fares in correct money. It must be pointed out at this point that conductors were not given a 'float' from the company and were expected to obtain enough change themselves prior to commencing duty. The official procedure for this situation was that the conductor was required to request the passenger's name and address, issue a ticket and submit an unpaid fare report. If the passenger refused to give their details they were asked to leave the bus. The problem with this was that the passenger was under no obligation to verify these details and accordingly many chose to offer a false name and address. It was often disputed whether LT ever wrote to the passenger to request payment. Where a particular passenger was suspected of deliberately and persistently offering a high value note, the details given and the place and time of boarding would be sent to revenue protection managers for plain clothes officials (Spots) to be deployed.

These were the days when many of London Transport routes covered an extensive area and fares were charged on a graduated system, usually increasing approximately every two or three fare stages (four to six stops) culminating in a maximum fare. Some passengers would often ask for the minimum fare and hope that the conductor would forget about them. As previously indicated when explaining **Rule 96 Excess Fares.** Many diligent conductors would return to the passenger and request the passenger to state another destination and charge them accordingly. Again, another minimum fare would be requested. Quite often the passenger was traveling the full extent of the route and hoping to reduce the fare by as much as they could. It was possible that by continually increasing the passenger's fare by increments the amount could be greater than if the passenger had requested the maximum fare at the start. Many conductors, myself included, were of the opinion 'If that's the game you want to play, I'm happy to continue charging you.' Unfortunately, in the days before 'Penalty Fares,' which will be covered later, it was not permissible to charge a passenger more than the maximum fare. Damn, foiled again!

These same passengers would often target a journey time when they knew that the 'Crew' would be relieved part way along the route and the conductor taking over would not be aware of the fare paid by passengers already onboard. However, London Transport in their wisdom had a procedure that was designed to negate this issue. You see, when a conductor took over a route mid-journey they were expected go through the bus saying 'Please have your tickets and fares ready' and were expected to 'Inspect' tickets already purchased. Sadly, over the years, a number of conductors failed to perform their duties as diligently as expected.

In my early days as a conductor, I would tend to take some fare avoidance incidents personally which, of course, is not advisable. One such incident occurred on a route 41 Routemaster bus in West Green Road, Tottenham. The bus was very busy and I was collecting fares on the lower deck of the bus. When the bus next stopped, I was aware of a young adult male who boarded and made his way to the upper deck. I gave the starting signal and continued with my duties. After two stops I had finished collecting fares on the lower deck and was making my way to the platform to go upstairs to collect the male passenger's fare, just as he was coming down to alight. I said' can I have your fare please.' At this point, the bus stopped and the male passenger smiled, gave me the finger and alighted the bus. Fare evader 1, Conductor 0. The next day I was on the same route and, at the very same location, I was aware of the same male passenger board the bus and make his way to the upper deck. This time, I did not give the starting signal, but immediately went to the upper deck and requested the passenger's fare. He handed me the correct money for his fare and held out his hand waiting for me to give him his ticket. Instead, I issued the ticket, which I detached from my Gibson ticket machine, and promptly screwed it up as I said 'That's yesterday's fare, can I have today's?' Now, this was not something that was endorsed or even encouraged by London Transport and, had this passenger become irritated, annoyed or even aggressive, I would not have had the backing of my GM (Garage Manager). To my surprise, the passenger smiled and said 'Fair play mate' and paid again. Honours even. Fare evader, 1 Conductor 1.

One particular passenger eventually became a 'marked man' amongst conductors on the route 243 after practicing his ploy on a regular basis. He would board the bus during the rush hour at Bruce Castle Park in Tottenham and make his way to the upper deck attempting to sit as near to the front of the bus as possible. He knew it would often take the conductor a few stops before they could ask him for his fare. He would then ask the conductor if the bus went to a different destination to those on the fare chart and when he was told 'no' would pretend he'd got on the wrong bus, apologise and immediately get off at the next stop. It was estimated that it usually took him two or three buses to reach his destination at South Tottenham station without paying a fare. He would also employ the same tactic on his way home in the evening. At this particular time the headway between each bus was no more than five or six minutes and therefore didn't cause the passenger too much inconvenience. Eventually a number of conductors alerted each other to this passenger and he would be stopped from boarding or asked for his fare before they rang the bus off. As this was in the days before penalty fares or a prosecution section it would have been extremely difficult for RPIs' or 'Spots' to prove to a court, beyond all reasonable doubt, that this constituted 'deliberate fare evasion.'

Driver/Operators

Driver/Operator (OPO) One Person Operated buses were being gradually introduced throughout London and although these buses required some minor adjustments for the purposes of ticket inspections, they eliminated a number of difficulties faced by RPIs'. Having already detailed how Conductors were expected to remain either on the platform or accompany the RPI around the bus as instructed, those involved in misdemeanours would blatantly ignore the RPI and scurry around the bus trying to correct any fare or ticket irregularities and/or disposing of evidence. The Driver/Operator was clearly deprived of this opportunity. When an RPI boarded an OPO bus they would instruct the driver to issue a printed waybill which would indicate the total register number at the start of the journey and the number of the next ticket to be issued. However, unscrupulous OPO drivers devised a number of different ploys to avoid detection by an RPI. Let's look at a few of these situations.

On many occasions a passenger might be struggling with bags of shopping which they would put down on the floor of the bus whilst they opened their purse or wallet to find the fare. Having placed the coins on the cash tray, they often would then be engrossed in putting their purse or wallet away and bend down to pick up their shopping. The driver on the look-out for this type of 'victim' will deliberately not issue a ticket if the passenger moves into the bus without realising one hasn't been issued. If further down the road an RPI boards the bus the driver will know that the RPI will encounter this passenger who will likely say that they must have forgotten to collect a ticket or that the driver did not issue them with one. As soon as the RPI has moved into the bus the driver will issue a ticket which they will detach from the machine and place it on the cash tray or nearby. When the RPI returns to question the driver, they will point to the ticket and say that the passenger left the ticket in the machine. Unfortunately for the driver this ticket would bear a number that has clearly been issued after the RPI boarded the bus. This irregularity/offence would also come under **B/R 90** and be known as, **Fare Taken-Delayed Ticket Issued**.

Another favourite of OPO drivers when spotting an RPI at the next stop would be to call a passenger back to the cab and issue a ticket before opening the doors, a tactic that would soon be restricted by the introduction of plain clothes ticket checking duties. Often this passenger would be a friend or family member (although not admitted or proven) who was allowed to travel free and been coached to tell an RPI that they got on at the last stop paid their fare and forgot to take the ticket. As the RPI observed this ticket to have just been issued (but could not prove that no cash had in fact been paid) this irregularity/offence would also be reported under **B/R 90 Fare Taken-Delayed Ticket Issued.** Compared to conductor operated buses, driver/operators were infinitely easier to covertly observe as every transaction took place in a fixed location at the front of the bus. More serious misdemeanours will be described in greater detail in the section dealing with 'Spots'.

OPO drivers were at this time using ETMs' (Electronic Ticket Machines) that were 'fixed' to the inside of their cab. A popular 'fiddle' was known as a 'two-five-eight' or blank ticket. When an ETM needed a new ticket roll the driver opened the top of the machine and inserted the ticket roll and fed the end into the rollers. To ensure the ticket roll was correctly inserted and ready for use the driver needed to press the buttons 2, 5 and 8 simultaneously (as these digits are always in a vertical line) with three fingers which fed a blank piece of paper the exact same size as a normal ticket and which would be torn off and discarded. This blank piece of ticket would however, always have a number of what would be the next ticket to be issued, in the bottom corner. So, in effect, if three blank tickets were produced, they would all have the same number until a new valid ticket had been issued. The unscrupulous driver would issue one of these from time to time and tell the passenger that the machine must have run out of ink but not to worry as it had registered and it has a ticket number.

In concluding this section there are times, on both conductor and OPO operated buses, when a passenger will claim that they had paid a fare and not been issued with a ticket. If the conductor or OPO driver confirmed that the passenger had paid but also stated that they were certain that they had issued a ticket, it was often possible for the RPI to collect all the tickets that had been issued on this journey from the other passengers (for example, ten fare paying passengers on board and only a total of nine tickets issued) and prove to the member staff that no ticket had been issued. This irregularity would be reported under **B/R 90 Fare Taken-No ticket Issued (FNT)** which on the surface appears to be a more serious offence than a Delayed Ticket Issued. However, on many occasions a conductor or OPO driver can be distracted by other passengers or incidents, which could often be corroborated by witnesses, and genuinely have forgotten to issue a ticket. In the eyes of an RPI or garage manager however, a member of staff immediately issuing a ticket to a passenger upon the sudden appearance of an RPI clearly indicates that they were indeed aware that no ticket had been issued.

You will no doubt be ready to move on from this section to the far more interesting, amusing, not to mention fascinating staff misdemeanours and fare evasion incidents. Nevertheless, the previous situations serve to illustrate the number and type of irregularities involving cash fares and the requirement and ability of an RPI to observe, investigate, assess and rectify the situation.

Incidentally, when OPO buses were first introduced the driver when pulling up at a stop was trained and required to open only the rear doors and observe that all the departing passengers had alighted safely before closing them and opening the front doors. Apart from safety reasons this also ensured that intending passengers could not board through the rear doors without paying or showing a valid pass undetected. As time passed bus companies began reducing the running times and drivers were often struggling to remain 'on-time' causing many of them to open both the front and rear doors simultaneously in order to speed up the process. This of course gave a number of people the opportunity to evade their fare.

PCO 'Spots' (Plain Clothes Officials)

For many years 'Spots' were a permanent, and considered elite section, comprised of experienced RPIs'. These individuals predominately worked in pairs and briefly put; their main duties were to covertly observe members of platform staff that had been suspected by their garage supervisors to be involved in misdemeanours. Many of these suspicions concerned revenue irregularities but could also include improper conduct such as smoking or consuming alcohol whilst on duty. The garage supervisor would fax over the name and badge number of the driver or conductor and his/her rota for the next two weeks. Spots would then be assigned to ride his/her bus on at least two or three separate occasions. The garage would not know which dates would be involved to avoid the driver or conductor being tipped off. A description of the driver or conductor was seldom sent as this alone could not be relied upon to positively identify the member of staff to be observed. This is where the role of uniformed RPIs', when carrying out routine ticket inspections, assisted 'Spots' by ensuring a member of staff was clearly displaying their I.D. badge and reporting them for not doing so. For many years 'Spots' would pay their fare in cash and would be allocated a 'cash float' on a monthly basis. All the tickets purchased by a 'Spot' would be accounted for by attaching them to their daily duty statement except where any were attached to a report as evidence and been sent to the relevant garage manager. In time, 'Spots' would be issued with 'All Zones Travelcards.' When boarding a bus and either paying a fare or showing a pass the 'spot' would be looking to see if the badge number matched that of the member of staff to be observed. Even though they had been given the bus route, running number and places/times of a journey they could not be sure if the intended member of staff had not, for instance, reported sick and a replacement had been assigned his/her duty. Once 'Spots' were satisfied that all the details were correct they would take up a convenient position/seat, where possible, but preferably not together, on the bus to observe the member of staff. As with RPIs' the most difficult member of staff to observe is a conductor. Unlike RPIs' 'Spots' must remain covert and therefore were not able to give the member of staff any suspicions or instructions. When operating on conductor operated double-deck buses a 'Spot' would often sit on the lower deck whilst the other would occupy a seat on the upper deck. The job required tremendous concentration. Once the 'Spot' had observed what value the conductors' ticket machine was set at it was possible to know by the way the conductor turned the fare selector dial whether the value was going higher or lower and matched what the passenger had asked and paid for. A 'Spot' would also be watching the conductor's every move in case the conductor was to surreptitiously reach into his/her uniform pocket and produce a previously issued ticket. If a 'Spot' suspected that the conductor had issued an 'incorrect' ticket he/she would wait until the conductor had moved to the other deck before approaching and identifying themselves to the passenger and ask to see the ticket and confirm what the passenger had asked and paid for. If the ticket was either for a lower value or a previously issued ticket and not issued from the ticket machine then the following procedure would be carried out.

This involved the 'Spot' immediately identifying themselves to the conductor and requesting a one pence (penny) ticket be issued and the number noted. This was a recognised break in the sequence of current fare values. The other 'Spot' would then be required to withdraw (collect) the ticket and request the passenger's details for their report. The conductor would be informed of the events observed and given the opportunity to comment. The conductor would then be required to issue the correct value ticket (referred to as 'issued under instruction') relating to the fare paid. A further ticket sequence always followed which was required according to accepted disciplinary guidelines. The conductor would then be informed of the offence/irregularity that they were being reported for. The 'Spots' would then go to the nearest revenue protection office and compile their report which would set out the events observed and comments made by both the conductor and passenger/s which would then be sent via internal mail to the garage manager of the member of staff reported.

'Smoking out' a 'Spot'

H aving earlier touched upon the type of offence and character of the individual member of staff liable to commit them on a regular basis it goes without saying that these individuals like any other persistent wrongdoers develop a keen eye and sixth-sense to those around them. They will generally be suspicious of anyone looking out of place for the area or time of journey. For this reason, 'Spots' must attempt to dress and act accordingly. One particular 'Trick' that a driver/operator or conductor, who was wary of a passenger, would be to light-up a cigarette to see if the suspicious passenger reveals him or herself. Being reported for smoking was generally not serious enough to result in dismissal and usually only warranted a written warning and was clearly preferable to being caught for a revenue-related offence. On one of my first assignments as a trainee 'Spot,' a driver/operator who was suspected of revenue-related offences lit-up a cigarette, I immediately reached into my pocket to pull out my I.D and plate and at the same time I caught the eye of my instructor seated opposite me who very slowly shook his head from side to side to indicate 'no.' Later in the journey the driver/operator re-issued a ticket to a female passenger and we immediately sprang into action. My instructor later confirmed that when we were engaged in observations on known or suspected revenue transgressors, we never acted on a lighted cigarette in case we were being 'Smoked-out.'

Total Evasion

I will finish the 'Spots' section with a few more examples of incidents in which I was fortunate to participate and best portray the diverse functions of the role. The first involves dealing with passengers who deliberately attempted to leave an open-back Routemaster bus without paying their fare. There are two important points which need to be borne in mind at the time of these incidents. The first is that London Transport had not yet developed its own Prosecution section and it was exceptionally rare for a passenger to be taken to court for a fare evasion offence. On these occasions LT relied upon passing all fare evasion incidents to British Transport Police who prepared the relevant paperwork and forwarded it to the Crown Prosecution section for their consideration. The second is that a passenger must actually step off the platform of the bus to be deemed to have avoided paying his or her fare. On a number of occasions, the revenue section would receive reports from conductors via their garage managers, which would detail the description of an individual who would regularly attempt to avoid paying their fare. The report would also include the boarding and alighting points as well as the days and times of the journey. With that in mind the following example will hopefully become clear. On these occasions two 'Spots' would be detailed to board and ride the bus from a few stops prior to the passenger's indicated boarding point. At this point we would not identify ourselves to the conductor (who on the day chosen may well not have been the conductor who had submitted the report.) We would try to sit separately at the back of the bus or as near as possible on the deck that the passenger was said to occupy. Once the passenger fitting the description had been identified we would watch as the conductor would hopefully continue to go along each deck collecting fares. Although as previously mentioned earlier in this book, conductors were expected to remember which passengers had paid and which had not, this however is not always foolproof and it remains the responsibility of a passenger to offer their fare to the conductor. The passenger would be watched to see if he or she perhaps pretended to be asleep or moved seats in order to outwit the conductor. When we were satisfied that the passenger had had plenty of opportunity and failed to offer his or her fare the following procedure would be followed. One 'Spot' would identify him or herself to the conductor and instruct the conductor to go to the deck involved and walk the entire length of the deck and back saying "Anymore fares" clearly and continually. The conductor would not be informed of whom we might be watching. This procedure was to confirm that the passenger had been observed to have been able to both see and hear the conductor requesting fares. Then when the passenger went to the platform prior to leaving the bus, we spots would also be on the platform. The reason that we could not identify ourselves and challenge the passenger at this point is that he or she could immediately say that they had just remembered they had not paid and had intended to offer their fare to the conductor before leaving the bus. Once the passenger had stepped off the bus we would identify ourselves to the passenger and inform him or her of our observations and caution the passenger before requesting the passenger's details and noting any statement made. You will have noticed that I said we would caution the passenger. PCOs' were the only bus officials with the authority to caution passengers at this time, although this was soon to be discontinued. Over the years especially when bus passes and travelcards became prolific London Transport devised a number of legal guidelines and procedures that subsequently had to be either abandoned or adapted to comply with the law. This was the case with the incident just described. It was pointed out that bus officials only had authority to demand a passenger's details whilst still on board a London Transport passenger vehicle. Later, I will describe a few more of these devised and abandoned procedures and the reasons why.

One for the road

An altogether different type of offence that I was once involved in was observing a driver/operator suspected of consuming alcohol on duty. London Transport/TfL has always been extremely conscious and diligent with regards to passenger safety. For many years drivers and conductors were recognised and rewarded for long periods of safe driving and conducting with certificates and badges. Any reports of unsafe or dangerous driving were taken very seriously and a DMI (Divisional Mechanical Inspector) would be sent out in plain clothes to ride the reported driver's bus and on rare occasions, when the driving standard was deemed to be too dangerous to be allowed to continue, even identify themselves to the driver at the next stop or safe place and instruct him or her to switch off the bus. We had been given information that the member of staff mentioned earlier was known to visit a local pub close to the garage during his meal-relief. Myself and a colleague had entered the pub minutes before the driver/operator was expected and ordered an alcoholic drink each which we had no intention of consuming. The reason for this was that two males' entering a pub and either not ordering anything or only ordering soft drinks might appear to be suspicious. For all we knew the barman or woman may be friendly with the member of staff and perhaps tip him off. A third 'Spot' was detailed to ride the driver's bus to the relief point and discreetly follow the driver into the pub in case he covered or hid his uniform and badge. Although we had no intention of consuming our drinks it will surprise many people to know that 'Spots' were at the time the only LT employees that were permitted to consume alcohol on duty in the following circumstances which even I find incredible today. The procedure that we followed was that one of us (known as number 1) had to be at the bar to be able to hear and see what drink the member of staff had ordered and order the same, in this case a well-known pint of lager. The driver/operator also ordered a meal. We had to watch and wait for him take a mouthful of the drink and then (number 1 'Spot') had to do the same. This was to verify that the drink the member of staff had consumed was indeed alcoholic. As bizarre as this might seem today this was the accepted procedure to follow in these circumstances. I, being number 1 Spot, then discreetly identified myself to the driver/operator and requested to speak to him outside in the company of my colleague where I informed him that he would be reported for consuming alcohol on duty. I reminded him that he was responsible for the return of his equipment and takings and to report to his garage manager first thing the next morning, whilst further adding, that as of this moment in time (which was documented) he was suspended from duty. Immediately afterwards we would telephone the driver's garage and inform a garage official of our actions and they would have to make arrangements to ensure that the driver did not attempt to complete his duty.

The Sting

A nother of these irregularities that 'Spots' occasionally dealt with involved using marked coins (with ultra violet pens) on Red Arrow services. These single deck buses, commonly known as 'cattle trucks' were high-frequency commuter services and operated between main-line London train stations such as London Bridge, Victoria and Waterloo. The buses were designed with just a few seats towards the rear and approximately two thirds of the bus was for standing passengers. They had a flat fare system and required the correct fare as the driver/operator had no interaction with cash and no tickets were issued. The system for collecting fares was via a unit known as a 'Johnson' box. These boxes were made of rigid clear plastic and secured to the door of the driver's cab. At the top of the box was a slot for coins and the driver/operator would be expected to check and confirm that the correct fare had been deposited and was then required to press a metal button on the floor of the cab with their foot which dropped (dumped) the coins into a sealed metal box inside the door of the cab which could only be unlocked by a garage official at the end of the duty. Revenue service's received information that one particular Red Arrow driver/operator had devised a system for gaining access to the coins deposited by passengers.

It transpired that this system was far from sophisticated or elaborate in fact it was not only simple in construction but incredibly effective. The member of staff had cut a long strip of rigid plastic from a laminated bus timecard and glued a flexible 'pocket' to the bottom end. Instead of continually 'dumping' the coins during the journey the driver/operator would allow the coins to build up and when the bus reached a terminus, he would dip the devise into the 'Johnson' box and wiggle it about until a coin would slip into the pocket and then be drawn back out. It would only take him a few minutes to extract £2 or £3 on each journey. I was one of a number of 'Spots' that were summoned to the office and given coins which we were required to endorse with our initials using an ultra violet pen. On the day in question the driver/operator was on route 501 and the plan was to have a number of 'Spots' along the route. Some of us were deployed on the journey towards London Bridge in order to maximise the amount of 'marked' money to be built up. When the bus left London Bridge I and the other 'Spots' were to board along the route and deposit our coins. When the bus reached Waterloo two senior officials were deployed to covertly observe the driver whilst the bus was on the stand which was at the rear of the station and out of sight of members of the public. The driver/operator duly performed his dishonest tactic. At this point the officials approached the bus and identified themselves to the driver/operator. The officials asked him if he was in possession of any money belonging to the company and he replied 'No.' The officials informed him of their observations and asked him if he was in possession of any coins of his own to which he replied 'Yes.' The driver/operator was asked to produce these coins and place them on a seat which he did. The officials then produced an ultra violet light (which was a small royal blue plastic box about the size of a small matchbox with a slim tube attached) which they proceeded to scan the coins with. A number of coins were identified and the driver was asked to explain how these coins came to be in his possession. Needless to say, at this point the driver knew the game was up and resigned before appearing at a disciplinary hearing. Frustratingly, I had retained one of these ultra violet devises which are now impossible to find, but which was accidently lost during a hurried garage clearance.

'Spot' the difference

Y ou are now going to observe two spots in action and at the end of the incident they are about to deal with you will be set a question. For this the reader is required to picture in their mind sitting on the lower deck of a double-deck OPO bus. Also sitting somewhere else on the lower deck are two 'Spots' who will both be watching intently every passenger who boards and alights the bus. Bear in mind also that 'Spots' are primarily interested in cash transactions (unless otherwise deployed) and must concentrate on (cash) fare paying passengers. The following sequence is the most basic possible for you the reader to fully comprehend.

It is important to also remember that at each stop a number of pass holder passengers may also be boarding the bus.

At stop 'A' a male passenger wearing a RED jacket boards the bus and pays the driver a fare. The driver issues a ticket to the value paid. The passenger detaches (takes) the ticket from the machine and goes to the upper deck. This passenger is in possession of the 'Check' ticket meaning the latest (correct) ticket issued.

At stop 'B' a female passenger wearing a WHITE coat boards the bus and pays the driver a fare. The driver issues a ticket to the value paid. The passenger does not detach the ticket from the machine (perhaps forgets) and takes a seat on the lower deck.

At stop 'C' a male passenger wearing a BLUE jumper boards the bus and pays the driver a fare. The driver fails to issue a ticket in respect of this fare and allows the passenger to take the previous ticket still attached to the machine. The passenger having detached the ticket from the machine then goes to the upper deck.

Clearly, we have three passengers that have paid cash fares and only two tickets have been issued by the driver.

The 'Spots' will wait until the driver closes the doors and sets the bus in motion. Number 2 'Spot' will go to the upper deck and identify him/herself to both passengers (wearing RED and BLUE clothing) and after explaining that they have done nothing wrong will collect (withdraw) their tickets as evidence.

Number 1 'Spot' will wait until the bus arrives at the next stop and immediately identify him/herself and instruct the driver not to open the entrance doors and to issue a one pence (penny) ticket. Number 1 'Spot' will inform the driver of what has been observed and number 2 'Spot' will have returned to the lower deck and handed their colleague the two withdrawn tickets. The reason for waiting until the next stop is that OPO drivers are required to complete all inspections of passes and cash transactions before closing the doors and proceeding to the next stop. If a 'Spot' were to identify themselves to a driver at the stop the irregularity occurred a quick-thinking driver could immediately issue a ticket and pretend he/she had just realised in time they had 'forgotten' to issue the ticket.

The driver will be instructed to issue a ticket to the value paid by the male passenger wearing BLUE clothing and this will be detached and retained by number 1 'Spot' as evidence (together with the two tickets withdrawn by number 2 'Spot.') All four tickets will have consecutive numbers as proof of the transaction sequence. The driver will then be instructed to issue a further three tickets which will be given to each fare paying passenger as replacements and their details requested. The driver will also be given a credit note to the value of the replacement tickets including the one pence ticket and informed of the irregularity/ offence they will be reported for.

Now for the question I told you to expect at the start of this chapter.

Would the driver be reported for;

- Re-issue of a ticket
- Fare taken-No ticket issued

The earlier pages of this book dealing with rules and examples of irregularities may help those of you who are not current or ex-staff to correctly answer this question which will be revealed on page 55 (no sneaking now) together with an explanation.

GOOD LUCK

NB: PCO (SPOT) SLANG;

Spots would often use certain slang words to avoid detection or arouse suspicion when operating in confined spaces such as, crowded bus stops, buses or cafes. Two of the most common being 'TOM' meaning a 'Ticket on Machine' as in the example given in relation to the lady (B) that leaves her ticket behind. Or when Spots, whilst randomly waiting for no particular bus, observed a driver or conductor with a 'TOM' on their ticket machine and would immediately board and ride the bus. The other word would be 'Tuesday' if they suspected they were being overheard when in conversation.

Gallery

All photographs from author's personal collection

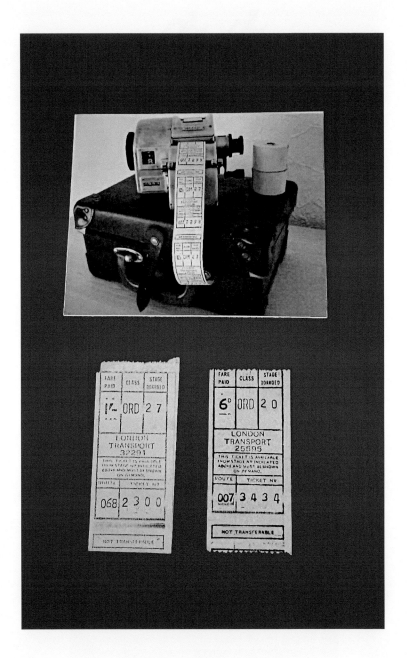

Gibson Ticket Machine and tickets

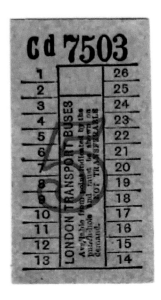

Emergency tickets. It was possible to re-seal the
E-Pack and not declare any used

	CLOSE Register readings	START Register readings	Quantity sold	code	Value (p)	AMOUNT £	p
E 6 1	**GIBSON** cash total sheet				*Please fold only where shown*	**MAY** **83**	
1				A	10		
2				B	20		
3				C	30		
4				D	40		
5				E	50		
6				F	15		
7				G	12		
8				H	1		
9				J	25		
10				K	22		
11				L	55		
12				M	3		
13				N	65		
14				P	70		
					TOTALS		

.... FOLD HERE ....

G.I. initials	G.I. duty number	Part/Final pay-in £ p	OFFICE USE	TOTAL		
		0 0	CONDUCTOR'S USE	PART PAID-IN	0 0	
				FINAL PAID-IN		
RECEIVED PART PAY-IN (amount in words)				TOTAL		
OFFICE USE	W/O Part Value		OFFICE USE	CREDIT		
				DEBIT		

NOTES

404/511 (1)

	Badge Number including Check Digit	Name (BLOCK letters)	If loaned, garage
Driver			
Driver			
Driver			
Conductor			

Machine Assistant's Initials	Conductor's Signature

Machine No.	Route No.	Duty No.

GARAGE......................................DATE....................19........

........TEAR OFF HERE........

	Badge Number Including Check Digit	Name (BLOCK letters)	Pay No.
Driver			
Driver			
Driver			
Conductor			

Garage ....Route No. ....Duty No. ....

Amount paid in ....Bonus................................

Garage Official's Signature..................................Date.....................19........

Conductors Waybill

Driver and Conductor PSV badges

ROUTE 192
ADULT FARES

FARES FOR CHILDREN
UP TO TWO CHILDREN under 5 years of age and accompanying a fare-paying adult or child passenger or a pass-holder and NOT OCCUPYING seats to the exclusion of fare-paying passengers are carried free.

Children aged 5 years and under 14 years, and additional children aged under 5 years are charged the fares shown on the child faretable except from 22.00 until last bus daily when adult fares apply.

Children aged 14 and 15 years are also charged the child fare (except after 22.00 hrs) but only upon production of a Child Rate Photocard.

CHARGES FOR DOGS
Dogs are carried at the discretion of the Conductor or Driver/Operator and are charged the child fare AT ALL TIMES.

Guide Dogs accompanying blind persons are carried free.

Dogs are not allowed on the seats.

TRAVEL PERMITS FOR THE ELDERLY AND HANDICAPPED
G.L.C. Travel Permits and London Boroughs' Handicapped Permits are available for free travel over the whole of this route at the following times:—

MONDAYS TO FRIDAYS	09.00*-00.59
SATURDAYS, SUNDAYS & PUBLIC HOLIDAYS	05.30 -00.59

*HANDICAPPED PERMITS are NOT valid MONDAYS TO FRIDAYS 09.00-09.30.

Concessionary Fare Permits issued by Hertfordshire County Council are available for travel at the child fare at the following times:—

MONDAYS TO FRIDAYS	09.00-00.59
SATURDAYS, SUNDAYS & PUBLIC HOLIDAYS	05.30-00.59

No other concessionary fare permits are accepted on this route.
THE FARES SHOWN APPLY ONLY WHEN THROUGH JOURNEYS ARE RUN

Stage Point No.																
33	**TURNFORD** Tesco's 33															
32	20	**BROOKFIELD LANE** Longfield Lane 32														
31	30	20	**FLAMSTEAD END** Jolly Bricklayers or **DEWHURST ROAD** 31													
30	40	30	20	**COLLEGE ROAD** Great Cambridge Road 30†												
29	50	40	30	20	**CHESHUNT** The Old Pond (or Council Offices S/B) 29											
28	60	50	40	30	20	**THEOBALDS GROVE** Station 28										
27	70	60	50	40	30	20	**WALTHAM CROSS** Queen Eleanor Statue 27†									
26	80	70	60	50	40	30	20	**BULLSMOOR LANE** 26								
25	80	70	60	50	40	30	25	25	**ORDNANCE ROAD** 25							
24	80	80	70	60	50	40	30	25	25	**ENFIELD HIGHWAY** Red Lion 24						
23	90	80	80	70	60	50	40	30	25	25	**BRICK LANE** Black Horse 23					
22	90	80	80	70	60	60	50	30	30	25	25	**PONDERS END** Southbury Road (or Enfield LT Garage) 22†				
21	90	90	80	80	70	60	50	30	30	30	25	25	**SOUTH STREET** 21			
20	90	90	80	80	70	60	50	30	30	30	30	25	25	**TRAMWAY AVENUE** 20		
19	100	90	80	80	70	60	50	30	30	30	30	30	25	25	**BOUNCES ROAD** 19	
18	100	100	90	80	70	60	50	30	30	30	30	30	30	25	25	**LOWER EDMONTON** Bus Station 18

CHILD FARES
See Reverse

(Rev. Jan 85)   ADULT (Herts) † Farezone

MAXIMUM OFF-PEAK FARE
A maximum off-peak fare of 65p is charged at the following times:—

MONDAYS TO FRIDAYS	09.30-15.59 / 19.00-23.59
SATURDAYS, SUNDAYS & PUBLIC HOLIDAYS	05.30-23.59

192
ADULT

Two convincing and two crudely altered passes

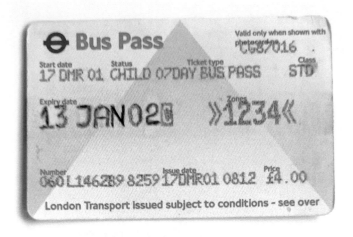

Altered bus pass. Original date dissolved using chemicals

One crudely altered and one genuine Red Bus Rover

Monthly
One Zone £10.70
Bus Pass

OUTER

TUE 19 NOV 85
WED 18 DMR 85

Valid only when
used with
Photocard No.   K2601

⊖

42 D634607

CHILD 7 Day
Two Zone £1.50
Bus Pass

INNER   OUTER

MON 18 NOV 85

From

SUN 24 NOV 85

Valid only when
shown with Child
Rate Photocard No.   EP491

£1.50 ⊖

38 N 678691

LONDON TRANSPORT
Travelcard
£352.00
ZONES
1 2 3a
CENTRAL INNER OUTER
Expires See over
Valid only when shown with Photocard No
£352.00 W'stow Cen A
Name.
Annual
00838
LONDON TRANSPORT
Travelcard
ZONES
1 2
CENTRAL INNER
Expires
See over
Valid only with Photocard No.
£52.00
Barbican
Name.
Quarterly
00115

Travelcard
LONDON TRANSPORT

£183.20

ZONES

1 2 3ABC

CENTRAL   INNER   OUTER

Expires   See over
Valid only when
shown with
Photocard No

£183.20

3 m...d   STANMORE

Period

Travelcard
LONDON TRANSPORT

£9.20

ZONES

3abc

OUTER

Expires   See over
Valid only when
shown with
Photocard No

£9.20   Stanmore

7 Day 01454

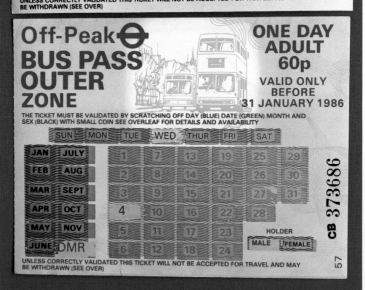

OUTER ZONE **3** ONE DAY **BUS PASS**

ADULT or ⊖
CHILD 80p
VALID ONLY BEFORE
31 JAN 89

THE DATE YOU WANT TO USE THIS TICKET MUST BE SCRATCHED OFF **BEFORE** YOU BOARD THE BUS. SEE OVER FOR DETAILS.

		SUN	MON	TUE	WED	THUR	FRI	SAT
JAN	JULY			1	7	13	19	25	29
FEB	AUG			2	8	14	20	26	30
MAR	SEPT			3	9	15	21	27	31
APR	OCT			4	10	16	22	28
MAY	NOV			5	11	17	23
JUNE	DEC			6	12	18	24

57 CB 091220

UNLESS CORRECTLY VALIDATED THIS TICKET WILL NOT BE ACCEPTED FOR TRAVEL AND MAY BE WITHDRAWN (SEE OVER)

Off-Peak ⊖
BUS PASS
OUTER
ZONE

ONE DAY
ADULT
60p
VALID ONLY
BEFORE
31 JANUARY 1986

THE TICKET MUST BE VALIDATED BY SCRATCHING OFF DAY (BLUE) DATE (GREEN) MONTH AND SEX (BLACK) WITH SMALL COIN SEE OVERLEAF FOR DETAILS AND AVAILABILITY

		SUN	MON	TUE	WED	THUR	FRI	SAT
JAN	JULY			1	7	13	19	25	29
FEB	AUG			2	8	14	20	26	30
MAR	SEPT			3	9	15	21	27	31
APR	OCT		4	10	16	22	28
MAY	NOV			5	11	17	23
JUNE	DMR			6	12	18	24

HOLDER
MALE FEMALE

CB 373686

57

UNLESS CORRECTLY VALIDATED THIS TICKET WILL NOT BE ACCEPTED FOR TRAVEL AND MAY BE WITHDRAWN (SEE OVER)

Scratch–off bus passes

Unpaid Fare Report – Driver copy

Date | D D M M Y Y | Time | H H M M

Route | | UFR **1110721**

Location | |

Passenger's home postcode | - |

Reason for issue (tick box and add details overleaf)

Confrontation ☐ | Vulnerable/in distress ☐

Other (reason must be given on other side) ☐

Unpaid Fare Demand – Passenger copy

Date | D D M M Y Y | Time | H H M M

Fare due | | UFR **1110721**

This form authorises you to travel on the bus on which it was issued. See the other side for ways to pay.

You must pay the outstanding fare within five days of issue.

⊖ Temporary Authority to Travel

Photocard not required **381426**

Rate:	Male	Bus Pass	LT Card	Goldcard
Adult/Child				
Youth/Privilege	Female	Rail only Season		Travelcard
				Peak / Off-Peak

Expires / / /

1 2 3 4 5 6 A B C D

Day Date Month Year

Valid by rail between

and

Issued by
Official no. | Initials | Date / /

Issued subject to conditions - see over

INSPECTOR'S DUTY STATEMENT

E

NAME G.WILLIAM. R NO. 3140 DUTY 3B AREA 2 SQUAD NO 1 MON DAY 22 OCT 1984

Point	From	To	Time engaged	How engaged	Remarks
SEVEN SISTERS STN	07:40	09:10	1-30	GENERAL SUPERVISION	HEADWAYS - IRREGULAR
SEVEN SISTERS STN	09:15	09:40	25	TAKING DETAILS ACCIDENT	
ST ANNS RD BRIDGE	09:58	11:33	1-35	QUEUE CONTROL	HEADWAYS - GOOD
STAMFORD HILL STN	11:50	12:20	30	RELIEVE INSPECTOR	HEADWAYS - GOOD
STOKE NWN CMMN	13:15	14:20	1-05	TAKING HEADWAYS	HEADWAYS - GOOD

Starting time 07:30
Finishing time
Spreadover time
Meal From / To
Total time worked
Unsocial hrs. worked
Timekeeping 4 40
Road control
Loadings
Checkings 2 19 25
Miscellaneous duties

WEATHER Morning DULL/DRY Afternoon DULL/WINDY Evening

GENERAL OBSERVATIONS AND SUGGESTIONS

DUE TO TRAFFIC LIGHT FAILURE AT JUNCTION - BROAD LANE - TOTTENHAM HIGH RD) DELAYS TO ALL SERVICES UP TO 15 MINS IN BOTH DIRECTIONS - 8:00 - 08:45

CONTROLLER PHONED 09:35 RE-ACCIDENT - INJURED PERSON REQUIRED MEDICAL AID

Route No.	Name	Number	Grade	Location	REPORTS (Offences and rule numbers to be stated)	CLASSIFICATION
253	T HARMER	65685	DVR	SF	ACCIDENT REPORT	
	B. SMITH	121212	CDR	SF		
73	C JONES	125701	CDR	AR	B/R 90 1x20° UNCOLLECTED FARE 1x50° CASH TAKEN	
149	A ROWE	64721	CDR	E	B/R 96 1x20° UNCOLLECTED) EXCESS FARE	

TICKET CHECKING SUMMARY

Type	Total Buses Checked	Total Tickets Checked	Passengers paying on alighting No.	Veh.	Unallocated fares Reports	No. Pssrs.	Cash	Excess fares Reports	No. Pssrs.	Cash	Undercharged fares Reports	No. Pssrs.	Cash	Tickets issued under value Reports	No. Pssrs.	Cash	Fares no ticket Reports	No. Pssrs.	Cash	Advised not reported Uni'd Fares	Over-riding	Ex's Fare	Cash
OMO O/D Split Entrance	2	40																					
OMO S/D Split Entrance																							
OMO Conventional																							
OMO Totals	2	40																					
CREW Totals	4	80			1	1	20	1	1	20													
TOTALS	6	120			1	1	20	1	1	20													

402/111 (1).05m 8/83 100 Stock)

Author's original training duty statement

OFFICIAL LONDON TRANSPORT 3207

Author's LT RPI badge

Author's TfL RPI badge

LT PCO (Spot) badge

Author's LT silver hall marked cap badge

Author's LT silver hall marked cap badge (reverse)

Author's TfL Gold badge

LT Medallion (Obverse)

LTB Medallion (Obverse)

LT Medallion (Reverse)

TfL RPI badge

Author in plain clothes (circa 2001)

Network Services

172 Buckingham Palace Road, London SW1W 9TN
Telephone: 01-222 5600 Extension:
Fax: 01-823 4900

Tel: 01-227 3810

TO WHOM IT MAY CONCERN

26 January, 1990

OFFICIALS AUTHORISED TO PRESENT CASES IN MAGISTRATES' COURTS
ON BEHALF OF LONDON REGIONAL TRANSPORT

This document is to certify that RONALD GWILLIAM is authorised to present
cases on behalf of London Regional Transport in Magistrates' Courts whose
jurisdiction covers areas where London Regional Transport bus services
operate.

Please afford Mr. Gwilliam the usual facilities in such matters.

G. Elliott
NETWORK SERVICES MANAGER, LBL

Registered in England and Wales Number 1900986,
Registered Office 172 Buckingham Palace Road London SW1W 9TN
VAT No. 238 7544 46
A subsidiary of London Regional Transport

Author's Court Authorisation letter

Revenue Protection Official

3207

 London Transport Buses

Transport for London

Ron
Supervisor

Transport for London

Ron Gwilliam
Assistant Revenue Protection Manager
Phone 020 7941 3419

Author with daughter Emma (left) and wife Sue (Sept 2013)

The Answer

FNT
FARE TAKEN-NO TICKET ISSUED

The reason is that for a ticket to be deemed to be re-issued it would need to be detached from the ticket machine. Whilst it is still attached to the machine it is not considered to have been issued to another passenger. So, to re-cap; the driver did issue a ticket to the first two fare-paying passengers (even though the second passenger did not take/detach their ticket) but did not issue a ticket to the third fare-paying passenger and allowed the passenger to take the ticket still attached to the machine. It is not the responsibility of a driver/operator to detach a passenger's ticket, with the exception of a ticket being issued by mistake or not required by the passenger (perhaps changing their mind or not having the fare) and in this instance the driver/operator would be expected to hand this ticket in at the end of the duty with the regulation 'Ticket Issued in Error' form in exchange for a corresponding reduction in takings.

In previous pages you will hopefully have remembered that I explained how some conductors or drivers might surreptitiously produce a ticket from their pocket which may have been picked up from the seats or detached from the machine by themselves and these once issued to another fare-paying passenger would be considered to have been clearly re-issued. Often these tickets would not be in numerical sequence with the other correctly issued tickets on this trip. Therefore, had the driver detached the ticket left behind by the second passenger and handed it to the third fare-paying passenger then this would have been a re-issued ticket.

Although the role of RPI still exist today, since the complete withdrawal of cash fares on London's buses the role of 'Spots' has been discontinued.

Report writing

RPIs' are trained in how to compile a detailed report. The crucial elements of a report were to relay the facts surrounding an irregularity or incident as concisely as possible. An RPI was not allowed or expected to express a personal opinion or suspicion, merely the evidence presented (tickets/ passes where offered) staff details, passenger details, journey details, coins/notes tendered, change (if any) received and any statements/comments made etc. Many reports could often follow a pro-forma example but on occasions more complex irregularities would require a more free-style report but still within the restraints detailed. These guidelines had been compiled by very experienced senior staff and generally agreed by local garage union officials and ensured that the garage manager, of the member of staff, receiving it could fairly uphold or dismiss the breach of rules alleged. Over time some aspects of report writing would need to evolve to embrace the changes in working practices but still retain the professional standards and appearance bearing in mind that for many years these reports were hand-written. The crucial opening line when describing the ticket or pass offered by the passenger went as follows; 'a male/female passenger seated lower/upper deck offered for my inspection' followed by the ticket/pass details. The word inspection confirms that the item in question had been examined and confirmed by a Revenue Protection Inspector (the clue is in the job title) to be genuine but incorrectly issued, not valid or fake. This became ever-more important when bus passes and travelcards became increasingly and more frequently used. Before long these items were being either misused, stolen, altered or copied and a passenger using such an item would try to disguise it by placing it in a pass holder or cover. It was often only by handling or looking at the reverse of a pass could a fake be detected. Not too long before I retired a training manager (who shall remain nameless) decided that perhaps report writing needed to be simplified. Sadly, the reason for this was because despite now being able to use computers, with both spellcheck and grammatical error facilities, the entry requirements for the role had been relaxed. The training manager had decided to replace the words 'offered for my inspection' to 'showed me.' I asked him why he had come to this decision and he smugly stated 'I don't believe in using four words when two will suffice.' I protested and argued against this flawed theory and asked if we would be changing the job title to Revenue Protection Show-person, but to no avail. I informed the manager that if we were going to simplify report writing and bearing in mind that we were 'London' Transport I had an alternative option and submitted the following:

SIMPLIFIED
(DUMBED DOWN) REPORT

Day/Date/Time/Route/Running Number/Place etc,

I approached a *geezer* (male) passenger sitting near the *apples & pears* (stairs) who showed me a *horse brass* (bus pass) which I spied with my *mince pies* (eyes) had been *son & daughter'ed* (altered). I said "Cor blimey mate, you ain't arf gonna cop it when you go before the *beak* (magistrate) I wouldn't be surprised if he fines you a *monkey* (£500). He said "I only used it cos I'm *brassic lint* (skint).

Sadly, the manager declined to take up my 'Cockney' suggestion. Clearly, the writing was on the wall (pun intended) and like many other areas of modern life, company standards were being sacrificed so as to be intellectually undemanding. As a very wise man once told me, it is far easier to require and maintain a high-standard than to allow it to be lowered and try to bring it back up.

In time, with the implementation of our own prosecution section (which will be covered in more detail) and the more serious offences as previously mentioned, regarding altered, stolen and fake bus passes and travelcards, RPIs' would be trained how to compile more legally binding reports such as police MG11 statements and documents and to be conversant with 'PACE' the Police and Criminal Evidence Act 1984. One of the important changes also involved RPI notebooks which now required them to have numbered pages and conform to the mnemonic No 'ELBOWS' which stood for no E-rasures, L-eaves torn out, B-lank spaces, O-verwriting, W-riting between the lines, and S-tatements must be in direct speech. This was extremely important when an RPI was required to attend court to give evidence and the defence Council could cross-examine them as to when they compiled their notes and how soon after the 'offence' they compiled their report. An RPI would often be expected to produce their notebook for examination.

At this point I would like to make it clear that although the previous examples described may appear to give the impression that the vast number of drivers and conductors employed by London Transport were up to no good this is of course very much the opposite case. The majority of platform staff were polite, courteous and diligent. Many of them would always be only too pleased to see an RPI or submit information to the revenue office about fare evasion incidents. As this publication is primarily about fare evasion and preventing financial loss to London Transport, I will continue with a few more examples where platform staff could, for example, be responsible due simply to being negligent or lazy. One such example is when the fares on a number of routes were either 50p for short to medium journeys or £1 for longer journeys. As the majority of journeys on these routes (I'm afraid to say I cannot give a more precise example) were short to medium, conductors would set their Gibson ticket machines to 50p which seems a very logical thing to do. However, some of them decided that instead of changing the fare value back and forth as required it was far simpler to issue two 50p tickets joined together to a passenger that asked for a £1 fare. Now, you might ask "what is wrong with this?" There is clearly no gain to be had by the conductor and no loss of revenue to LT which is of course true. However, on a few occasions two regular passengers, possibly couples or friends, would board the bus together and soon saw an opportunity to save one or the other some money. The idea would be for one of them to ask for two 50p fares (which would be reeled off joined together by the conductor) when one passenger would be taking a 50p journey and intending to leave the other passenger, who was taking a £1 journey, with both tickets after alighting the bus. If an RPI boarded the bus after this had happened, they would not be able to dispute the second passenger's claim that they had paid for a single £1 fare and these are the tickets that the conductor had issued him or her. If the conductor could not remember the passenger this could not be disputed. In this instance the fare evader would have avoided detection. The tickets would be retained by the RPI and the conductor would be instructed to issue the passenger with a £1 ticket and would be reported (unfairly) for **B/R 90 Alleged Incorrect ticket/s issued**. If done knowingly and admitted by the conductor the same procedure and report would be carried out minus the word **Alleged.** This might seem a minor irregularity but unwittingly the conductor has assisted in the loss of 50p to LT. Multiply this a good many times and you appreciate the extent of losses possible. Two other problems associated with this 'simple' error is that when ticket machines and waybills are audited and surveyed they corrupt the data needed to plan future bus frequencies and destinations, not to also mention, that when you consider the huge amount of tickets being unnecessarily duplicated this represents an even greater cost in paper and ink to London Transport.

Another example of a conductor unwittingly costing LT/TfL lost revenue can be explained as follows: On many long routes (before flat fares) the fares were graduated and could range from 30p to 90p or more. An RPI might approach a passenger who was taking a 90p journey but could not offer a ticket for inspection and claiming that the conductor had not been round to collect the fare yet. At the point of inspection, the passenger had by now taken a 50p journey. On a number of occasions, the conductor would claim that the passenger was a regular passenger and that he/she would have collected the fare before the passenger had completed they're journey. The conductor would be instructed to collect the 90p fare and issue the passenger a ticket. The conductor would be reported for **1 x 50p fare uncollected- 1 x 90p cash taken.** The reason for this instead of **1 x 90p uncollected fare** is that it is true that the conductor would/could have collected the fare as stated. However, LT/TfL in their wisdom would explain that had the passenger not been taking their regular journey that day, as assumed by the conductor, the passenger could have left the bus without paying whilst the conductor was engaged elsewhere on the bus, an amount (50p) that could at that point be proven as potentially lost.

Having made it clear that some conductors could unintentionally lose TfL revenue, two other completely intentional ways would firstly be, that by deliberately tearing off a previous ticket from the machine by pulling it sharply to one side, resulting in the next ticket coming out 'scrunched up' and ensuring the value could not be read clearly. The conductor having now set the machine to a lower value than that paid. Secondly, it was possible to claim that the ticket machine had jammed, then opening the emergency ticket pack whilst failing to correctly account for the various colour-coded value tickets made of thin card.

Delayed Ticket Checks

There came a time, when many bus passes, travelcards and elderly persons travel permits were being stolen, altered or misused and one of my favoured tactics would be to board, where possible, a double-deck OPO bus at a terminus whilst the bus was on the stand. I would obtain my checking ticket and inform the driver/operator that I would be doing a 'delayed ticket check' after a few stops. I usually only did this when I knew the driver/operator was one of our more trustworthy members of staff. Then I would sit in a corner seat at the back of the lower deck and observe the passengers as the bus pulled onto the first stop. Although this was best done when in plain clothes, I have even done it when in uniform by tucking my hat under my arm whilst seated. I would pay particular attention to those passengers that boarded and showed the driver a pass. From my position I could not always be sure whether it was a bus pass or travelcard, for example, but would make a mental note of whether it was in a wallet or bus pass holder and what colour it was. I then observed where the passenger put it on their person as they entered the bus, whether it was in a back or front trouser pocket or in a jacket or shirt pocket for example. After one or two stops, I would then walk to the front of the bus and commence my ticket inspection. Most passengers would be too engrossed in what they were doing and not even realise that I had already been on the bus. Experience also tells you that most fare evaders or persons of questionable character prefer to sit on the upper deck and usually look out of the window to see if a ticket Inspector is getting on. This would give them the time to run down the stairs and leave the bus. On a good many occasions a passenger with an invalid pass and has been surprised at your sudden appearance 'out of nowhere' will usually tell you that they bought a ticket and now can't find it or that the driver didn't issue them one. Now, in normal circumstances this would usually need to be investigated with the driver thus giving the wrongdoer the chance to leave the vehicle. But when you have observed the passenger to show a pass when they boarded you knew full well that there was something wrong with that pass. It was always amusing to watch their face when you told them where they boarded the bus and that they have, for example, shown the driver a pass in a black plastic pass holder which is in their back trouser pocket. The passenger often couldn't work out how you knew this and would carry on denying it and sometimes turn out every other pocket in order to convince you otherwise. On these occasions I would simply say 'Can I see the pass you showed the driver which is (pointing) in *that* pocket.' This tactic often produced results that would otherwise have gone undetected. TfL (having superseded LT) did not encourage this tactic. Like so many industries they seemed more interested in quantity rather than quality and thought this type of ticket inspection would take longer and fewer buses would get checked. At this particular time, I would describe myself as a somewhat pro-active rebel and strongly disagreed.

I spy with my little eye

In my introduction to this book, I explained that since the introduction of oyster and credit card payment systems and the complete withdrawal of printed passes and cash tickets the visual detection skills of the RPI have become defunct. Let me now expand further on the art of visual detection perfected by many vastly experienced RPIs.

Most travelcards and bus passes were printed on a mixture of paper and card with black ink. The most obvious and easiest way to alter the dates would be to go over them with either a ball point pen or pencil and in some cases a common 'John Bull Printing Set' which were widely sold in most stationary stores. On many occasions numbers would be cut from other expired passes and simply stuck over another.

It wasn't always simply the dates that would be altered but also the period and zonal availability offered. There was a time when travelcards were printed with three London zones numbered 1, 2 & 3 and coloured Blue for Central London, Green for Inner London and Orange for Outer London accordingly. The reason for colour coding the zones was to help bus staff visually ensure that passes were valid in that zone whilst concentrating also on the dates. These travelcards were printed on paper which was then adhered to a piece of card. It was possible to hold a pass over the spout of a steaming kettle which would, after a few minutes, lift and separate the paper from the card which could then be glued over another travelcard with less availability.

Experienced RPIs developed a skilled eye, in a similar fashion to an art expert, who could often tell at first glance that something didn't look quite right and on closer inspection could determine that a pass had a slightly incorrect font, shade of colour or thickness for example. Another mistake made would be incorrect date abbreviations such as DEC instead of DMR for December or MAR instead of MCH for March. As in many other industries an RPI's performance would be monitored by KPIs' (Key Performance Indicators) which broke down how many and which types of offences or irregularities were detected. When it came to altered or forged travelcards or passes RPIs' would take pride in comparing how many in any one period they/we had 'spotted.' I would often say...'Yes, but we will never know how many we might have missed.'

An often-used excuse by an adult caught with a crudely altered pass was to say that one of their children must have taken it from their jacket or wallet and drawn on it. Unfortunately, this excuse failed to prevent them being taken to court as it is deemed what it is known as an 'absolute' offence and does not require London Transport/TfL to prove whether it was used knowingly or not. This was referred to by the police as using a 'forged instrument.'

With the advancement of computer technology, the war against fare evasion was destined to become a far more professional, sophisticated and organised battle for RPIs' to adapt to.

School for Scoundrels

Fare evasion had now moved on from free-hand inventive instruments of deception to computer-generated counterfeit masterpieces. Some of the most prolific 'Factories' turning out these items were colleges and schools. Before the introduction of free travel for schoolchildren and students there was a significant increase in many of these cases being traced back to places of education. Schoolchildren often accounted for a large percentage of fare evasion cases. Prior to the more serious development of forgery and counterfeit travel documents there were many instances of school pupils or students over the age of fifteen using child bus passes or requesting a child fare. This was very difficult for drivers, conductors or RPIs' to establish the correct age of a young person, as we all know, they come in various shapes and sizes. There was also no requirement for them to carry proof of age. As you can imagine, many of the most difficult ages to gauge were those between fourteen to seventeen and one of the simplest questions to ask someone who appeared older would be 'What is your date of birth?' The problem with this was that for many it was simply a case of changing their year or when only just over the age, the month. I decided to have a list of dates and star signs and when suspicious would then ask 'What star sign are you?' This proved a question too far for a good many. As previously mentioned when dealing with early cases of fare evasion, school children like many adults, would often deliberately offer a coin or note that they hoped the conductor couldn't change. Fortunately, this often tedious, battle of wits was somewhat alleviated by the introduction of child photocards and ultimately free travel for all under 16-year-olds.

Another visual awareness skill developed by RPIs' when checking passengers' tickets was to also scan the movements of other passengers as you worked your way through the bus. It was possible to observe that someone was looking nervous or fidgeting or whispering to a companion for example. If a passenger seated further back suddenly got up to exit the bus an RPI would be expected to ask the passenger to show a valid ticket or pass as they approached them. This was all the more important on an OPO bus as all passengers on board would be expected to have either paid their fare or shown a valid pass to the driver upon boarding. One of my own examples of this was when I was checking tickets on the top deck of an OPO bus which was still at the stop where I had boarded. I noticed an adult male talking to two slightly younger-looking females whilst they were seated together on the rear bench seat. The male then got up to go past me and I asked him to show me his ticket or pass. The male showed me a valid travelcard and I allowed him to go down the stairs and assumed that he had alighted the bus. Within a very short space of time, whilst I was still checking towards the back of the upper deck, I heard a male voice behind me say 'excuse me' and I moved aside to let this passenger pass. It was not necessary to suspect or ask any passenger at that point to show you a ticket they were clearly entering the bus knowing you are checking tickets. However, as this male passed me, I noticed it was the same male that I had just checked and as he approached the two females' I noticed him hand one of them two cash tickets. Before challenging them, I went back down to the driver as he was closing the doors and asked him if he remembered the male passenger that just came down and asked for two cash fares. The driver said 'yes, he got on with two girls and they all showed passes, I thought that was strange?' I went back to the upper deck and asked the three of them for their tickets or passes. The male again showed me his valid travelcard and the girls showed me cash tickets. I then said to the girls 'can I see the passes that you showed to the driver.' At first, they denied having shown passes and I informed them of what I had seen and what the driver had told me. It transpired that both the girls had child rate bus passes despite one of them being eighteen and the other nineteen years of age. I withdrew the child rate passes, obtained their details and submitted the relevant reports to my office. The male passenger was re-imbursed for the cash tickets and the driver given a credit note. It was not possible to report the male passenger for aiding and abetting fare evasion as this was very difficult to conclusively prove to a court.

It's a Fare Cop

M any years prior to my becoming an RPI, it was virtually unknown for a bus passenger to be taken to court and prosecuted for fare evasion. The reason for this was that in the days of cash only fares not only was it extremely difficult to prove a passenger intended to evade their fare, RPIs' could only request a passenger's name and address but had no means of verifying this and had no authority to demand it. Add to this that in the days before mobile phones and bus radios for communication it was not possible to summon the assistance of the police. The subject of the police was further complicated by the fact that the Metropolitan Police did not view fare evasion as a particularly serious offence and the British Transport Police only responded to incidents involving rail and underground stations. On the odd occasion when a passenger admitted fare evasion and provided their correct name and address these details were forwarded to the BT Police offices and they, after interviewing the RPI, would submit the facts to the Crown Prosecution Service for consideration. With the gradual introduction of travelcards and bus passes and the increase in fare evasion incidents, the time taken and high failure rate for successful prosecutions would ultimately lead London Transport to establish their own Investigation and prosecution section and this will be covered in greater detail later.

The relationship between TfL and the Metropolitan Police underwent an extensive transformation over the next forty years of my service resulting in a dedicated transport policing unit. This would include RPIs' attending Hendon Police College to help develop an understanding of bus related offences and to develop a strategy for future joint operations. Initially these static exercises were arranged to target routes where not only was fare evasion highest but police intelligence indicated that both local and non-local gangs were using buses to bring drugs and weapons into the area. Without this knowledge, the reader, like many others, may well have thought that this was something of a sledgehammer approach to crack a nut (the nut being to save a low value bus fare) this was of course far from the truth. As well as stolen and forged travelcards, bus passes and credit cards often being recovered, individuals with outstanding warrants were apprehended. One problem was that at times buses were being held and delayed while the RPIs' or police officers were dealing with passengers. Another problem was that local people were using social media to alert each other to avoid those routes or areas. At one intelligence meeting, later in my career as a manager, I suggested that plain clothes RPIs' and police officers should board a bus (two stops prior to where uniformed police officers were waiting) and the bus allowed to proceed. Once a number of individuals had been checked and suspected they were taken off the bus immediately at the stop selected. This meant that there was no delay to the bus. After an hour or so the team would move to another nearby location to intercept any persons hoping to circumvent being detected. Not only was this tactic highly successful it also ensured that there was both a covert and high visibility presence in the areas.

Operation
'Artful Dodger'

S ome two and half years after my appointment to RPI the revenue section took part in a combined operation involving London buses, London underground and Network Rail South West at Waterloo station, called Operation 'Artful Dodger' on 13 May 1987. The operation was designed to 'Blitz' every form of transport coming into and out of Waterloo station. To my knowledge, it remains the only such exercise of its kind and size and featured on the TV news programmes that evening. This can still be seen if the reader types in 'Waterloo Station, Fare Dodgers' on 'You Tube.' The eagle-eyed of you should be able to spot 'Yours Truly' amongst the assembled array of 'Ticket Inspectors.'

At this point, to emphasis the extent of fare evasion that has evolved since the invention of computerised technology, I would also reference the investigation by Alan Selby of the 'Sunday Mirror' a few years ago. Mr Selby travelled by train from Waterloo Station to Guildford and back again using a fake travelcard obtained on the 'Dark Web' by his investigative team. Mr Selby describes how the travelcard fooled barrier staff who he described as 'Highly trained' to spot fakes (echoes of my own experiences of knowing how many we successfully detected, but not, how many we must surely have missed) including the on-board conductor. Mr Selby went on to describe that the metallic strip on the reverse of the travelcard did not work but because staff admitted that they 'often go on the blink' he was allowed through the barriers. 'At no point was I challenged on the validity of the ticket which, to all but the expert eye, looks utterly genuine' Mr Selby said. A rail fraud investigator at the time when shown the fake travelcard said 'I must say it's very good, far better than many I've seen. It's good quality on old ticket stock. There are two slight anomalies on the ticket that you might not pick-up.' In response at the time, The Rail Delivery Group, an association of rail companies, said 'Fare Dodgers deprive us of £200 million pounds every year.' Mr Selby confirmed that his team used an encrypted email service to ask for a quote. A representative of the seller called 'Paul' wrote that they only work with Bitcoin. The seller had hundreds of reviews on his site. The ticket purchased duly arrived a few days later by Royal Mail with a Manchester postmark. In addition, the report stated that one such operation in Bournemouth Dorset, that had been running for seven years, had been 'Busted.' The ringleader was a fifty-one-year-old Taxi driver who previously worked for South West Trains. He offered open-ended railway tickets to order using blank ticket stock and a printer. Mr Selby's report went on to say that criminal gangs from abroad are also now supplying the British market. Mr Selby's full report can still be viewed online.

The 'Scratch-Off' Bus Pass

Amongst the many different types of passes and tickets that were valid for use on London's buses, I single-out the famous 'Scratch-Off' bus pass for special mention for two contrasting reasons. The first; is that it was without doubt a quite brilliant marketing invention. The beauty of it was that passengers, especially those that only travelled occasionally, could purchase them and keep them unvalidated until the day required and thus negated the need to stop at a station or newsagents to buy a day pass. The pass was validated by scratching-off the day, date and month of travel required. Later versions were printed without the day, due to many passengers innocently scratching-off the right day but not date or vice-versa which were then refused for travel. Some passengers did this deliberately hoping to use them for two days by insisting it was simply a mistake. The second; was that this pass caused further problems for RPIs'. The first of these was that some passengers would deliberately make the tiniest of scratches on each section. When inspected and told that the day, date and month needed to be fully revealed a number of these passengers would blatantly refuse saying 'I have scratched it' and refuse to hand it to the RPI. Some of these passengers would become quite obstinate or aggressive causing a stand-off that often involved a delay to the bus and a possible assault situation for the RPI. This was becoming an everyday occurrence across Greater London and more so in areas where fare evasion was already high. I decided to raise this at the next managers meeting and suggested that RPIs' be issued with hole punches similar to those used by National Rail companies and that a hole be punched in all three sections of the pass. Furthermore, any passenger refusing to have their pass validated in this way could legally be asked to leave the bus. My suggested recommendation was duly accepted and became standard procedure. The second problem that these passes caused was that they became increasingly popular amongst passengers that regularly used stolen and forged travelcards, bus passes and elderly persons Travel Permits. The culprits would buy a scratch off bus pass and carry this with them unvalidated at all times. The reader needs to bear in mind at this point that many passengers could make any number of journeys and not encounter an RPI. The beauty of this pass from their perspective was that if an RPI did board the bus, rather than show them the illegally used item, they would swiftly validate the scratch off bus pass and show this to the RPI. As I said earlier, a quite brilliant marketing idea appreciated by both honest and dishonest passengers alike, not so much by RPIs'!

Lastly on this subject, referring back to the earlier part of this book when I described the often ingenious, laughable or lamentable ploys employed by the travelling public to avoid paying their fare, the following example using a scratch off bus pass surely fulfils all three, if not, then certainly the first two: It was reported by one RPI that a lady had devised a system whereby she placed three black paper dots over each section of the scratch off bus pass, which she would rotate accordingly, and placed it in a clear plastic wallet thereby giving it the appearance of having already been inspected by an RPI. However, the RPI stated that something didn't look quite right and asked the lady to hand him the wallet, and as she did so, one of the dots fell off!

From Caught to Court

A short time prior to my appointment to Revenue Protection Inspector in October 1984 a small number of SRPIs' (Senior Revenue Protection Inspectors) had been seconded to set up an investigation and prosecution section. This was initially known as FIPS (Fraud, Investigation and Prosecution Section) and later IPS having been advised due to legal advice to drop the word 'Fraud.' The early process would start with RPIs' submitting a report and any evidence in the form of a bus pass or travelcard which would be along lines of the following example:

Day/date/time…

Route Number…Running Number…Destination…

Driver/Operator/Conductor Name/Number

Irregularity…Out of date Bus Pass

I approached a male passenger who I now know to be Mr John Doe of 14 Smith Road, Tottenham, N15 (which was verified by a library ticket) seated on the upper deck who offered for my inspection a seven-day bus pass serial number 123456 which was dated to expire 27 May 1985 for his journey from St Anne's Road to St Marks Church a fare of 70p. I observed that the pass was two days out of date. I said 'Is this the pass that you are using for your journey?' He said 'Yes, I meant to get a new one today but I forgot.'

In these early days there was no formally standardised pro-forma requirements so long as most of the deemed relevant facts were in the body of the report. If the passenger could not provide any form of verification (remembering that it was prior to modern technology and a voter's list check for example) the report would slightly differ as follows: I approached a male passenger who gave his name as Mr John Doe of 14 Smith Road, Tottenham, N15 etc. in these cases the FIPS/IPS Section would send out a V letter (verification) asking the passenger to respond and confirm or give any other reason for using an out-of-date bus pass. If no reply was received within 14 days this was added to a list of names and addresses for Investigating SRPIs' to follow-up by calling at the premises. This type of report and process would not conform to modern day legal requirements but just like the earlier staff report regarding consuming alcohol on duty these would often be deemed sufficient to secure a successful prosecution. During my initial RPI training we were shown an example from one established RPI who after describing the journey details would always write…'I spied with my eagle eye that the pass was out of date'…or…'I spied with my eagle eye that the pass had been altered' depending on the type of offence. As highly amusing as this was it clearly wouldn't be acceptable today. The next step would be to arrange and issue a summons for the passenger to attend court. An SRPI would attend court to present the case. As this was a summary offence there was no need for a legally qualified court presenter. I still have my letter of introduction which informs the courts that I was authorised to present cases on behalf of London Regional Transport.

Newsagents

It may surprise a good many people to know that apart from forged or counterfeit bus passes and travelcards the second biggest cause of revenue loss to London Transport was from shops acting as Pass Agents of which some unscrupulous newsagents were the biggest culprits. As you might no doubt be aware when, at that time, a newsagent sold a bus pass or travelcard they received a percentage of the sale and were required to keep meticulous and up to date records. So, how did this happen you may well ask? From time-to-time newsagents like many other businesses would have a break-in or burglary. When it comes to newsagents the most popular items stolen include cigarettes, alcohol and cash. If they are a Pass Agent then bus passes and travelcards are also very desirable. However, not all break-ins or burglaries are genuine and even when they are it must be remembered that like most other businesses, newsagents can claim insurance for items reported as stolen whether genuine or merely alleged. In respect of bus passes and travelcards a very clever and deliberate deception came to light. Before revealing the scam perpetrated by the newsagent the following needs to be explained. After such an incident a newsagent would report that a batch of passes had also been stolen when in fact they had not. Once notified,

London Transport would record these batches as stolen and the serial numbers would be noted and relayed to revenue staff. As previously stated throughout these pages, in the days before RPIs' equipment became fully computerised these lists would be in paper form and had to carried about the person. It was clearly not possible to memorise all these numbers and on busy buses, especially in rush hours, it was not possible to constantly pull out these lists every time a pass was presented for inspection. Many RPIs' would devise their own methods in the hope of detecting some of these passes such as concentrating on any pass that had a serial number starting with a sequence of numbers that they found easier to memorise. Now, back to the newsagents. After some considerable time, the newsagent after being re-stocked by London Transport, would start selling the alleged stolen passes to their customers except this time instead of only receiving a percentage of the price they would pocket the full amount. In one particular area an extended family owned more than one news agency and the alleged stolen passes were distributed via the other outlets. Once a pass that had been reported as stolen was found by an RPI to be in the possession of a passenger it was important not to assume that the passenger had anything to do with the theft or that they had knowledge that the pass was in fact stolen. The passenger would be told that there had been an issuing error that needed to be corrected etc. Once a passenger's details had been obtained and verified and asked where the pass had been purchased a plain clothed revenue official would be sent to the newsagent to purchase a bus pass in the hope of being sold a stolen pass and further strengthen the case against the offending agent.

Staff and Dependent Passes

B us drivers and conductors are issued with staff passes that allow them to travel on all London Transport bus and tube services (this was later extended to certain rail companies) and were also entitled to obtain a dependent's pass on behalf of a wife, husband, partner or child. These passes may only be used by the person they are issued to and like all travel passes and tickets are not transferable. These passes were first issued, to staff only, in the days when many bus staff had no personal means of transport to enable them to travel to their depot and take-over points. These benefits were later extended to include a family member in a bid to compensate for less favourable pay rates at the time. Sadly, London Transport, like many other employers, would find that a small number of employees would seek to abuse these generous benefits. One way of doing this would be to 'rent out' their pass to another family member or friend who's travel cost could effectively be halved to the benefit of both parties. In the main it would work in a couple of ways. One would be that the member of staff would use their own transport to reach their depot when on duty and likewise mostly when traveling off duty. Another way would be that a member of staff when going to and from work would board a bus in uniform with their PSV badge on display knowing that other bus conductors or drivers would naturally assume that they had their staff pass on them but saw no need to ask them to produce it (which they were required to do) as any member of staff not in possession of their staff pass was required to pay their fare like any other passenger. A member of staff's uniform and PSV badge did not entitle them to free travel. These staff passes were valid for use both on and off duty. The non-member of staff using the staff pass would be assumed to be travelling off duty in their own clothes or those that worked in other non-uniformed departments. Staff passes were of course issued together with a photocard which often, in these situations, would have a photograph of the perpetrator stuck over the original. It was also possible for a member of staff to falsely report that they had lost their staff pass and for a fee of ten pounds receive a replacement, meaning that there were now two staff passes bearing the same name in use.

Over the years many bus conductors and drivers either leave the industry or are dismissed and a number of them fail to hand in their staff pass reporting them as lost or stolen. Likewise, their PSV badge and uniform. These are all recorded and the details circulated but as previously mentioned, prior to today's modern technological advances, this required relying on printed paper list or an exceptional memory.

Night buses

P rior to 1984, the year I was promoted to Revenue
Protection Inspector, RPIs' were never required to work
nights. In those days there were only three shifts which
comprised of early, middle and lates. Early duty was 06:00hrs
to 13:54hrs, Middle Duty was 10:00hrs to 17:54hrs and Late
shift was 14:00hrs to 21:54hrs. The reason for this was that
night buses were primarily provided for workers in industries
such as newspapers, postal services, railways, bakeries or office
cleaners. These were the days before night clubs and extended
pub licensing hours and most late bus route finishing times of
around midnight were deemed sufficient for those enjoying
a night out, at the cinema or pub, for example. Night buses
in those days ran every night with the exception of Saturday
night/Sunday Morning. I had been a night bus conductor on
route N90 from 1979 to early 1984 which ran from Waltham
Cross in Hertfordshire to Pimlico in London. During this
time almost all, night bus passengers were regular working
folk and depending on which journey was being performed
myself and the driver would know who we would be picking
up and at which stops. As time progressed the boom in night
clubs and late-night dining and pub licensing hours, especially
on Saturday nights, prompted the need for these services to

be extended to seven nights a week. Not surprisingly, night bus staff were now being confronted with ever increasing numbers of drunk and disruptive passengers who knew full well that there were no ticket inspectors at night and zero chance of being caught fare evading. To make matters worse gangs of youths were now roaming around London at all hours on buses looking for trouble not to mention fights breaking out amongst drunks. Before long it became apparent that as passenger numbers increased so did the amount of fare evasion and anti-social behaviour. By 1985 all night buses were now OPO (One Person Operated) and drivers were reporting that large groups of passengers in Central London were opening the rear doors and piling into the bus. It was decided and announced at a meeting of managers and RPIs' that a pilot scheme exercise involving RPIs' and City of London police should be carried out at Trafalgar Square on a Saturday night, where many night bus routes leaving Central London served. This was so successful that it was decided to arrange further exercises when the relevant resources could be provided. As previously stated, at this time RPIs' were never required to work nights compulsively and therefore whenever these exercises were planned volunteers were sought. As time went on it became clear that there was a need for night revenue inspectors Pan-London and not just at weekends. From this the 'Night Squad' was born.

At one of these subsequent meetings, having volunteered on a couple of previous occasions and not been selected, I made my feelings known and that I had also noticed that the same RPIs' were being selected. Bearing in mind that I was still a relatively new and inexperienced RPI, this caused the hairs on the back of the neck of one particular manager to bristle at this thinly veiled accusation of favouritism and he said 'Mr Gwilliam, checking tickets on night buses can be very intimidating and completely different to checking tickets on days.' I already knew when I became an RPI that this manager and I were unlikely to get along. In reply to his comment, I addressed him by name and said "I'm not sure if you are aware of my staff record with London Transport but before I became an RPI, I was a night bus conductor for over four years and checked and collected passenger's passes and fares without the assistance of approximately twelve police officers." This was greeted with howls of laughter from all the RPIs' assembled. The reader might not be surprised to learn that our working relationship never did recover or improve.

The Night Squad

The Night Squad initially started with an SRPI and six RPIs' (all volunteers) to be seconded for three months in plain clothes to ride around London and the adjoining suburbs in an unmarked Ford 7-seater van. The night team was selected with at least one RPI from each area so that there was always someone with an intimate knowledge of the area and routes being checked. The plan of action would be for the RPIs' to be dropped at a bus stop just ahead of an approaching night bus which they would board and begin ticket checking whilst the bus was allowed to continue on its journey with the 'Night Van' following. Once the RPIs' had completed their ticket check they would alight the bus, return to the night van and move on to another nearby bus route. The advantage of the RPIs' being in plain clothes was that they could also mingle unnoticed at busy bus stops, particularly in Central London, and actually watch and listen to passengers discussing their intended scam such as one passenger boarding the bus, showing the driver a pass and then dropping it out of a window to their friend. Or one passenger distracting the driver whilst their companion slips through behind them unnoticed. This allowed the RPIs' to prioritise which passengers they checked first, informing them of their observations. The rota was designed so that each

RPI and the SRPI could rest for two nights of each week. As time progressed and bus radio communications improved, along with the introduction of mobile phones, bus drivers could contact Centrecomm (LT/TfL's control centre) and request the night squad to attend or intercept their bus if they had or suspected fare evasion situations. The problem here was that if the night van was in north London it was not practical or possible to drive all the way to a route in south London and vice versa. It needs to be also remembered that members of staff could be capable of taking advantage of passengers who may be slightly inebriated or tired after a long night out and perhaps not issue them a ticket, issue them a ticket left behind by another passenger or short change them, for example. One particular night bus driver came to the attention of the night squad after making an unusual number of calls to Centrecomm asking if the night squad was in the area, as he suspected he had fare evaders on board. Each time the night squad were able to attend, the driver would say that the passenger or passengers had alighted. It so happened that after a while an RPI from that area of London knew of the driver and that he had been suspected of ticket irregularities in the past. It was suspected that the driver's tactic was that when he was told by Centrecomm that the night squad was not in the area he felt safe to defraud the company in various ways or means. A plan was hatched that the next time the driver contacted Centrecomm they were to inform him that the night squad was not in the area and could not attend when in fact they were and could. As you may well have guessed, sure enough the plan worked, he was reported for a number of irregularities and after a disciplinary hearing, dismissed. Over the years it was clearly evident that more than one night van was needed and was therefore enlarged with a permanent squad of RPIs' of which, I would eventually become the Senior Supervisor.

Bendy Buses

I liken the introduction of articulated buses, commonly known as 'Bendy Buses,' to the 'Scratch Off' bus pass, in as much as, on the surface, they appeared to be an advantageous addition to the benefit of the travelling public. However, unlike the 'Scratch Off' which came to cause some unintentional and unforeseen problems and issues for revenue protection staff, the 'Bendy bus' brought with it a number of clearly foreseen issues to anyone that either used or worked on public transport, particularly in inner and Central London. Articulated buses were first introduced in London in October 2001 for a trial on route 207 between Shepherds Bush and Hayes-by-Pass using Volvo B7LAs Volvo B10LAs hired from Hampshire & Dorset and First Glasgow, respectively. In short, the perceived advantage was that by using a longer vehicle and utilising the front and middle doors the buses were capable of carrying more people and speeding-up the boarding and alighting process, trusting the passengers to validate their oyster or credit cards by using the 'Readers' situated throughout the bus. An additional advantage was that the driver had no interaction with passengers. In June 2002 new Mercedes-Benz Citaro 0530Gs were introduced on Red Arrow services 507 and 521 in Central London and eventually to many other routes.

Prior to these articulated bus trials, a number of 'Open-Boarding' trials were carried out on selected conventional OPO routes. Not surprisingly, fare evasion increased on those particular routes. It became somewhat amusing in as much as I once joked that I thought a secret button had been inserted on the top step of the upper deck and that as soon as an RPI stepped on it a number of ejector seats were triggered. However, it appears that a decision had been taken and the widespread use of articulated buses went ahead. The reader will probably not be surprised to learn that many people did not validate their Oyster or credit card and simply sat or stood as close as possible to a reader. When an RPI boarded the bus, the passenger would simply 'Tap-in' and claim they had only just boarded. Even when a plain clothed RPI boarded the bus as soon as they were seen to be checking tickets the majority of passengers throughout the bus still managed to validate their cards.

Eventually, it became clear that a team of RPIs' would be required on any one bus to cope with the amount of people failing to validate their oyster and credit cards. Once again, I became instrumental in devising a plan of action that was to at first, 'catch' and later 'deter' passengers from employing this practice. Simply put, a number of plain clothed RPIs' would board the bus and stand by each of the readers. Then at an arranged time and signal the RPIs' would place their back against the reader, display their I.Ds. and announce "Have your tickets and passes ready for inspection" and in the process, preventing and intercepting those that made a last-minute dash to validate.

Bendy buses were also later introduced on some night bus routes and as a sad reflection of our times they started to attract many homeless people who would simply ride around on them all night. Many of them would even bring a blanket or duvet with them and stretch-out on the rear bench seats. Many people of course would have sympathy for these individuals and think that this was perhaps a harmless situation that should just be ignored or tolerated. The trouble here was that drivers were concerned that when the bus reached a terminus these people could not or would not leave the vehicle which meant that the driver could not check the vehicle for either lost property or damage to the bus which is part of their responsibility before starting their next journey. Many drivers, particularly females also felt unsafe when parked on a deserted bus stand in outer London in the middle of the night. Add to this that many regular passengers would complain about hygiene issues and demand that these people should be removed which would often involve the police being called to which they were often reluctant or unable to attend.

Articulated buses were finally withdrawn between July 2009 and December 2011.

The Martini
Inspectors

There was a time when revenue services were being asked to assist in a growing number of both revenue and non-revenue duties. I duly, jokingly, dubbed the section then as the 'Martini Inspectors,' (for those of you old enough to remember) the TV advert for the famous tipple went…'Anytime, anyplace, anywhere.' The following are a few of these such duties.

AIRBUS AND RIVERBUS SERVICES

It may surprise people to know that for a time around the late 1980's and early 90's RPIs' and 'Spots' were employed to ride and check both Airbus and Riverbus services where fares were considerably higher than on conventional bus services.

SECURITY SQUAD

Also, around this time there was a worrying increase in criminal damage, primarily graffiti, being caused to buses at night whilst parked on garage forecourts as well as gangs of youths either firing air guns or stoning buses as they travelled through some inner and outer London housing estates. The latter becoming so serious that many drivers were refusing to operate these services. Naturally, their union reps were fully behind them and informed the bus companies concerned that unless something was seen to be done then they would instruct all their drivers to boycott these routes. The police were the obvious first port of call and they promised to increase patrols in the areas affected but, as you might well suspect, as soon as the police showed up the gangs dispersed only to return moments later. Not only that but due to the increase in more serious crimes the police simply could not provide the necessary resources required to alleviate the problem and satisfy the concerns of the bus companies. It was decided that plain clothes RPIs' in unmarked vehicles may be able to 'Stake out' the areas most affected in the hope of providing the police with descriptions of youths and their movements, and a number of joint exercises were conducted which after a time were successful enough to reduce and eventually eliminate the problem to the satisfaction of both the bus drivers and the bus companies. Similarly, these same RPIs' were deployed to covertly observe the bus garages affected by criminal damage, often discreetly sitting on buses during the night with the intention of challenging, deterring and providing descriptions of the offenders which were immediately circulated to the police.

The Security Squad would often work with plain clothes police officers in areas where staff assaults were becoming a growing problem. These RPIs' were selected for short secondments which allowed regular RPIs' and 'Spots' to concentrate on fare evasion duties.

DIVERSION DUTIES

As you can imagine, in both Central and even outer London, a great many events take place that require the surrounding streets and roads to be closed. This is where NTCs' (Network Traffic Control) officials are responsible for implementing and signposting diversion boards to assist bus drivers etc. Many of these events such as Remembrance Sunday, Royal Occasions and Pride, for example, require additional staff to supervise, advise and ensure that members of staff and the public are kept informed of diverted routes and alternative means of travel. Once again, this falls to RPIs' to make up the numbers.

Penalty Fares

The London Regional Transport (Penalty Fares) Act was introduced in 1992. Initially the maximum penalty fare was set at £5 for buses and trams (£10 for underground and rail services.) Prior to this there was effectively no sanction for passengers that were 'Overriding', either the conductor on crew buses was expected to collect any additional fare (which was previously explained) and could not exceed the maximum fare. Like-wise an RPI. In the case of a conductor operated bus, where the conductor had failed to collect this, the conductor would be instructed to collect the additional fare and issue another ticket. The conductor would then be reported for B/R 96 Uncollected excess fare, as also previously documented. In the case of a One Person Operated (OPO) bus, the driver/operator could not be expected to issue any excess fares and therefore RPIs' were issued with Excess Tickets books. The passenger would be required to pay the additional (excess fare) and the RPI would issue the passenger with the top copy of the excess ticket (which was white) duly detailing the destination and amount, and the RPI would retain the copy (which was yellow) and became known as 'Yellow Perils'. The RPI would then pay the excess fare to the driver and request a ticket to that value, the RPI would staple the ticket to the copy which in turn would be attached to their duty statement. Clearly, for passengers who regularly and intentionally overrode their fares there was more to be gained and little or nothing to be lost. Although these Penalty Fares became, incorrectly, described as an, 'On the Spot Fine,' it was in fact not. Penalty fares are a civil debt, not a fine and are used to discourage casual fare evasion.

TATTS (Temporary Authority to Travel)

A t the time of the introduction of travelcards, bus passes and travel permits it was never envisaged that these passes would ever need to be withdrawn, let alone replaced. However, as the incidents of passes being misused began to increase it was decided that an RPI could (in as few words as possible) legitimately withdraw a passenger's pass as evidence, if it was proven or admitted to have been misused to avoid the fare. Unfortunately, a number of offences arose that would later become legally challenged. For example, a passenger who admitted deliberately travelling beyond the availability (in this case, area or zone) of their pass. An RPI would be required to withdraw the pass, obtain the passenger's details and inform them that they would be reported for (out of zone) fare evasion. The prosecution process is clearly lengthy and it transpired that although the passenger had misused the pass, on the particular day in question, they had paid for and were therefore entitled to use the pass within the valid area or zone for the rest of its valid days/dates. As a result, it was deemed that they had been deprived of it by this procedure. Another problem, was when an issuing agent (usually a newsagent) had incorrectly dated a pass (either, incorrect dates, too many days or too few) for example, and where the passenger was deemed to be unaware and the pass withdrawn. In light of these cases, it was decided that RPIs' should be able to issue a replacement pass and submit the original for investigation. In the case of misdated passes by newsagents they would be contacted and advised or investigated as to the reasons why?

This facility could also allow an RPI to assist a vulnerable child or other member of the public in distress, that may need to make a number of bus journeys to reach home, and therefore had a beneficial use. Many years later when I was a night RPI a number of females that had been to various bars or nightclubs, would go to Charing Cross, City of London, police station and claim that they had lost their purse or had it stolen and were unable to get home and were thereby stranded in London. The police, aware that there were night RPIs', would call Centrecomm and request us to attend and issue these individuals with a pass to get them home. Unfortunately, these calls began to increase, particularly at weekends, and it was clear that the 'word' had got round and many of these individuals were simply not genuine and were after a free journey. We had to inform the police that we were unable and not obligated to constantly attend for this purpose.

A touch of humour
– Just the ticket

During my years in revenue services, I often felt the urge to inject a touch of humour to the proceedings from time to time and I reproduce here three such examples:

The first is a spoof report of a night bus inspection in which one such encounter relates to the characters of the highly popular TV and film franchise 'Star Trek' as follows...

STAR TREK
EVASION OF THE FARE CATCHERS

Statement of RPI 3207 Ron Gwilliam

On Monday 23 April 2001, I was in full uniform in the company of RPIs' 3104, 3234, 3232, 3120 and 3414. We were being followed in the transporter (Night Revenue Van) commanded by AAM (Acting Area Manager) Alex 'Talk to Me' Whitmey.

At 23:15 hours, we boarded a route **N1701 Starship.** 3234 and 3414 stayed on the lower deck, 3120 and 3232 went to the upper deck, myself and 3104 went to the **Holo Deck.**

I approached a male passenger who I now know to be **Captain James T. Kirk** who offered for my inspection a **LaForged** travelcard serial number 123456. I said "Is this the pass you showed the Pilot" Mr Kirk said "Yes"

I said "This travelcard is a photocopy" Mr Kirk said "I know, I've made a number of them, this is **Seven of Nine**"

I said "So this is quite a little **Enterprise** you've got going" Mr Kirk said "Yes"

I said "Can you let go of the pass please" Mr Kirk said "I'd like to **Klingon** to it a bit longer"

I said "If you don't let go, I'll do a **Red Alert** and make no **Bones** about it" Mr Kirk said "Can't I just pay a penalty fare and I'll send a **Checkov"**

I said "No, I also want your photocard" Mr Kirk said "My what?" I said "Your photocard mate" Mr Kirk said "Oh, you mean my **Picard"**

I said "I want your name and address" Mr Kirk said "Ok, I'll tell you" I said "Go on then I'm all ears" Mr Kirk said "Hello **Spock** I didn't recognise you"

I said "Don't be funny mate"

He gave me his name and address and said "Are you aware of the **Data** protection act" I said "Your particulars are safe with me, sir"

But before I could verify these details, Mr Kirk said **"Beam me up Scotty"** and disappeared.

The second is a spoof Revenue Protection Notice (in place of the official notice) that informed RPIs' that the V&A (name and address verification) system was currently unavailable.

REVENUE PROTECTION
NOTICE 0001/2012

To: All Revenue Protection Inspectors
From: Ron Gwilliam; Senior Supervisor Operations
Subject: Temporary PDA FIX

As you are all well aware, we have been experiencing serious software problems with the new system. In response to the many RPIs' that have complained, calling the new 'Crown' system 'S**t', we have decided to replace the letter 'C' with the letter 'B' and until the 'Brown' system has been 'fixed' have decided to replace it with a temporary new system called P.I.G.E.O.N (Processing Individuals Generated Ensuring Operational Normality)

With immediate effect each RPI will be issued with two types of Pigeons. (a) Common Pigeon, for inner London and (b) Wood Pigeon, for checking out in the sticks (outer London.) Both Pigeons must be attached to your utility belt in an upright position. This is required under H&S and RSPB guidelines.

When dealing with an irregularity you must attach the passenger's details to the appropriate Pigeon and release it from any exit or window. The Pigeon will travel by the most direct route to the roof of Palestra where a member of the Business Systems team will verify the details and send the bird back to you (this may take approximately one hour but you will appreciate that this is much quicker than the present system.)

Like the 'Crown' system the 'Brown' system can fail. Your Pigeon may crash due to either flying into a highly polished window or receiving an air gun pellet whilst in flight. You will be alerted to incoming messages by a loud 'Coo Coo'ing' sound.

Any Pigeon delaying the return of data by stopping-off for any 'Lovey Dovey' antics will be dismissed from service. Supervisors have been advised to avoid doing static police exercises at Trafalgar Square and Peckham.

THE THIRD IS EXPLAINED
IN THE TITLE.

DECK OF CARDS (Adapted from the 1959 hit record by
Wink Martindale)

During the summer of '85' a number of young A/RPIs' were waiting to be assessed. Those A/RPIs' that had a revenue manual took them out and read them, but this one young man had only a deck of cards and he spread them out. In due course a supervisor spotted the young man and said "Son, put away those cards" and he was put on a charge (DP1)

When the A/RPI was brought before the Revenue Manager, the manager said to the supervisor, "Why have you brought this A/RPI before me." "For playing cards at an assessment, sir" said the supervisor. "And what have you got to say for yourself son." said the manager. "Much sir" replied the A/RPI. The manager said "I hope so, for if not, I will punish you more than any A/RPI was ever punished." The A/RPI said "Sir, I have been on duty since early this morning and I have neither a revenue manual nor a procedures book. But I hope to satisfy you sir, with the purity of my intentions." And with that the young man started his story. "You see sir, when I see the **ACE** I'm reminded that there is but one Revenue Services." "And when I see the **2** I'm reminded of the route that goes from Marylebone to Crystal Palace." "When I see the **3** I'm reminded that there are three managers to whom I must at first report, The Training manager, the Revenue Protection manager and the Area manager." "And when I look at the **4** I also think of the Investigations manager." "When I see the **5** I'm reminded that there are five areas in which I might be sent to work, NE, NW, SE, SW and Central." "And the **6** reminds me that the VNA system is down and not to try again for at least thirty minutes." "When I see the **7** I'm reminded of the number of days in a week." "When I look at the **8** I'm reminded of the number of rest days in a month." "And when I see the **9** I'm reminded that it's often quicker to dial two more than to wait for Centrecomm to answer a Code Red."

"When I see the **10** I'm reminded of the number of TATTS in a book." "And when I see the **Jack** I'm reminded of all those A/RPIs' that jacked it in and how they all now envy me."

"When I look at the **Queen** I'm reminded that I'm on diversion duties and there is still no sign of the NTCs' that I'm supposed to be *assisting*." "When I see the **King** I'm reminded of the 'No Smo-King' signs on buses." "There are two **Jokers**, one of whom is in charge of deployments." "When I count the number of **Diamonds, Hearts, Spades and Clubs** on a deck, I find that there are **365**, the number of days in a year." "There are **52** cards, the number of weeks in a year." "There are **12** picture cards, the number of months in a year." "There are **13** tricks, the number of pay periods in a year." "There are **4** suits, one for each of the Managers to wear."

"So, you see sir, my deck of cards serves me equally as a revenue manual, procedures book and calendar." And friends, the story's true, I know…I was that A/RPI. The moral of this story is, if you're going to bulls**t…practice…practice…practice!